hebrew tracing

letters

מכתבים בעברית

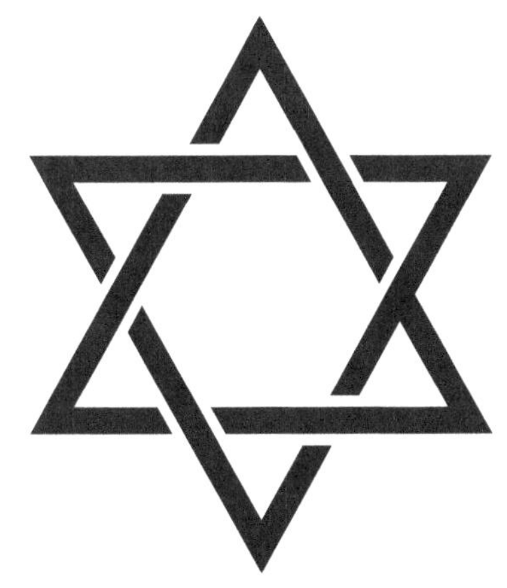

by wolfeyesqueen

2020

this book bleongs to :

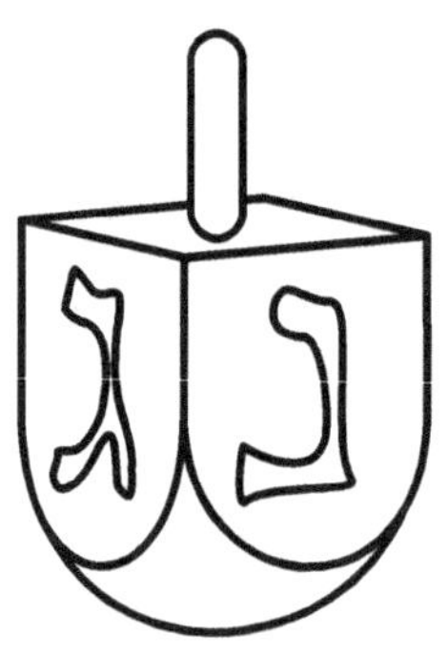

- name :

- last name :

- address :

- email :

- phone :

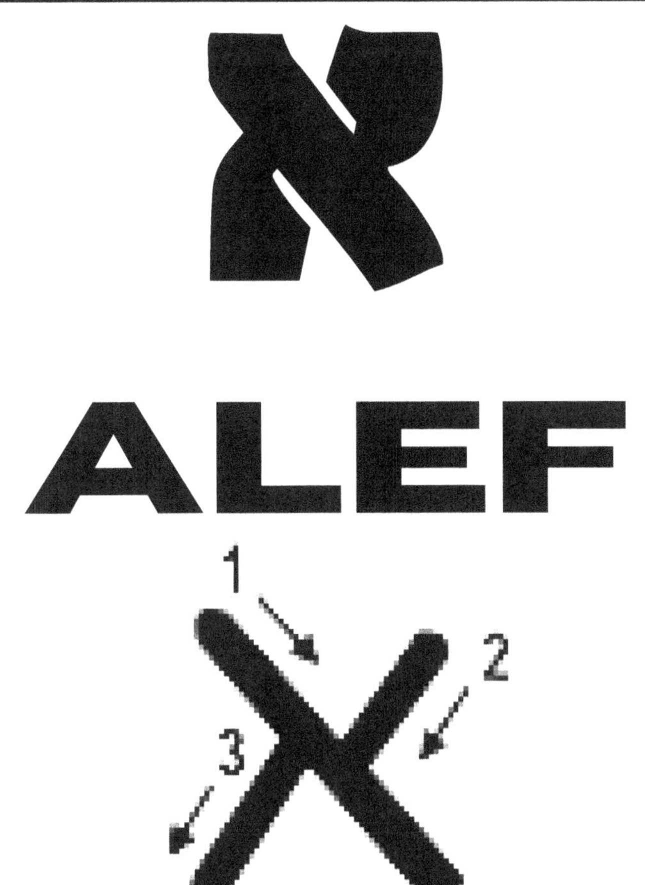

ALEF

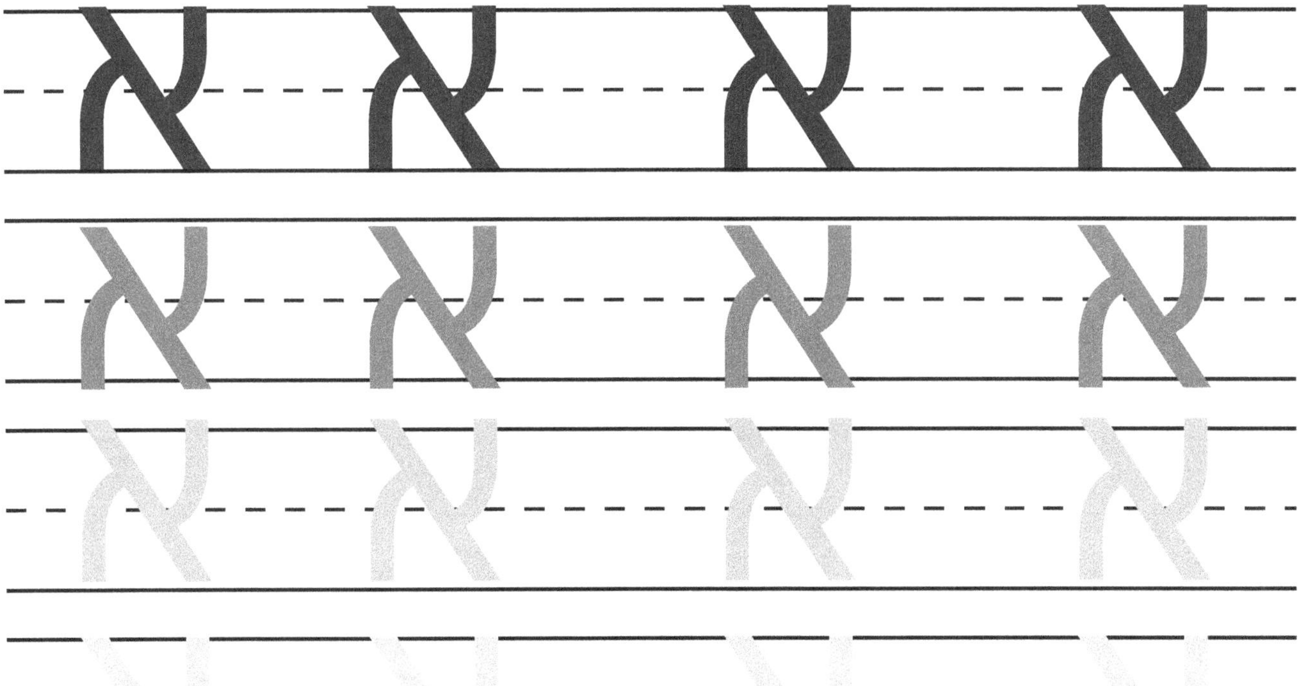

BET

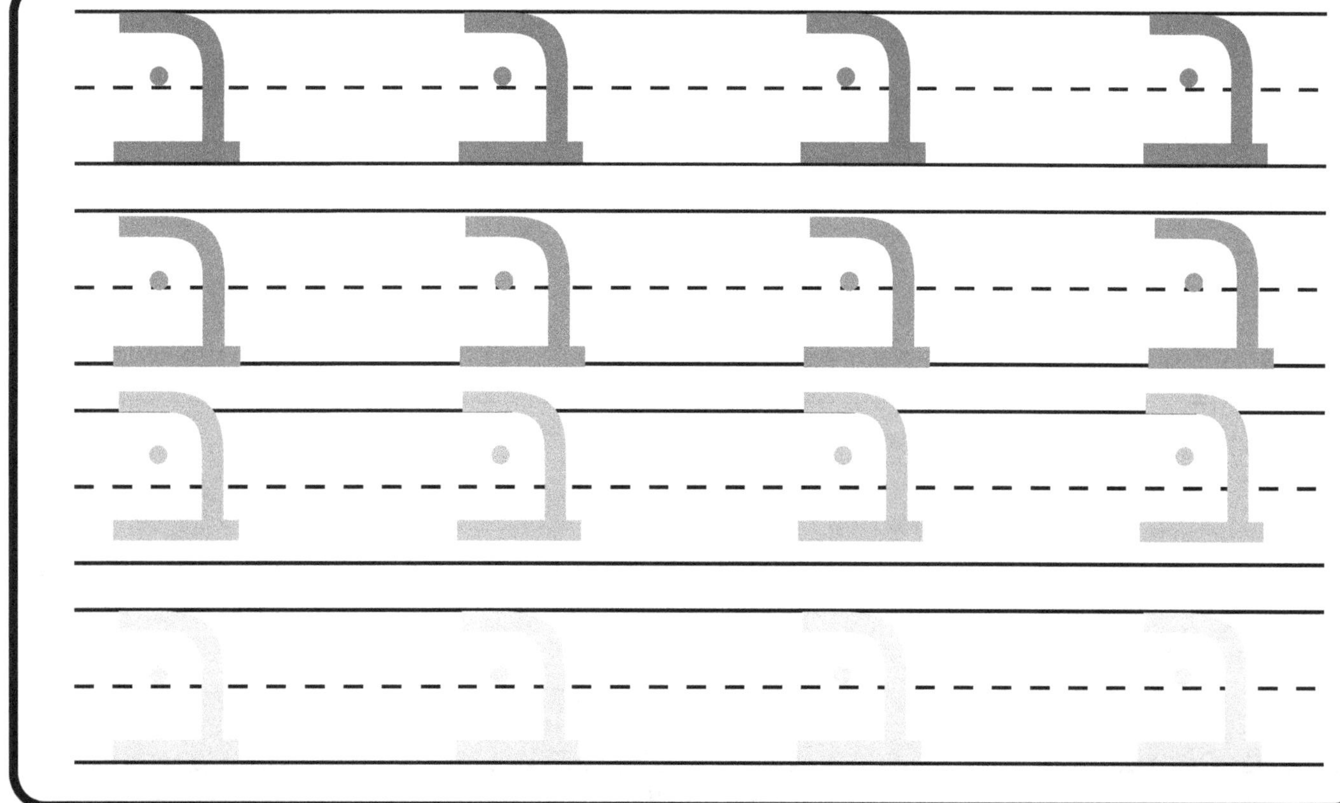

בֿ

VET

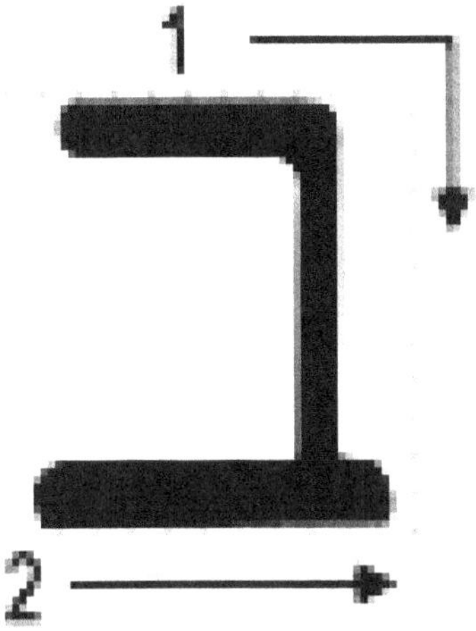

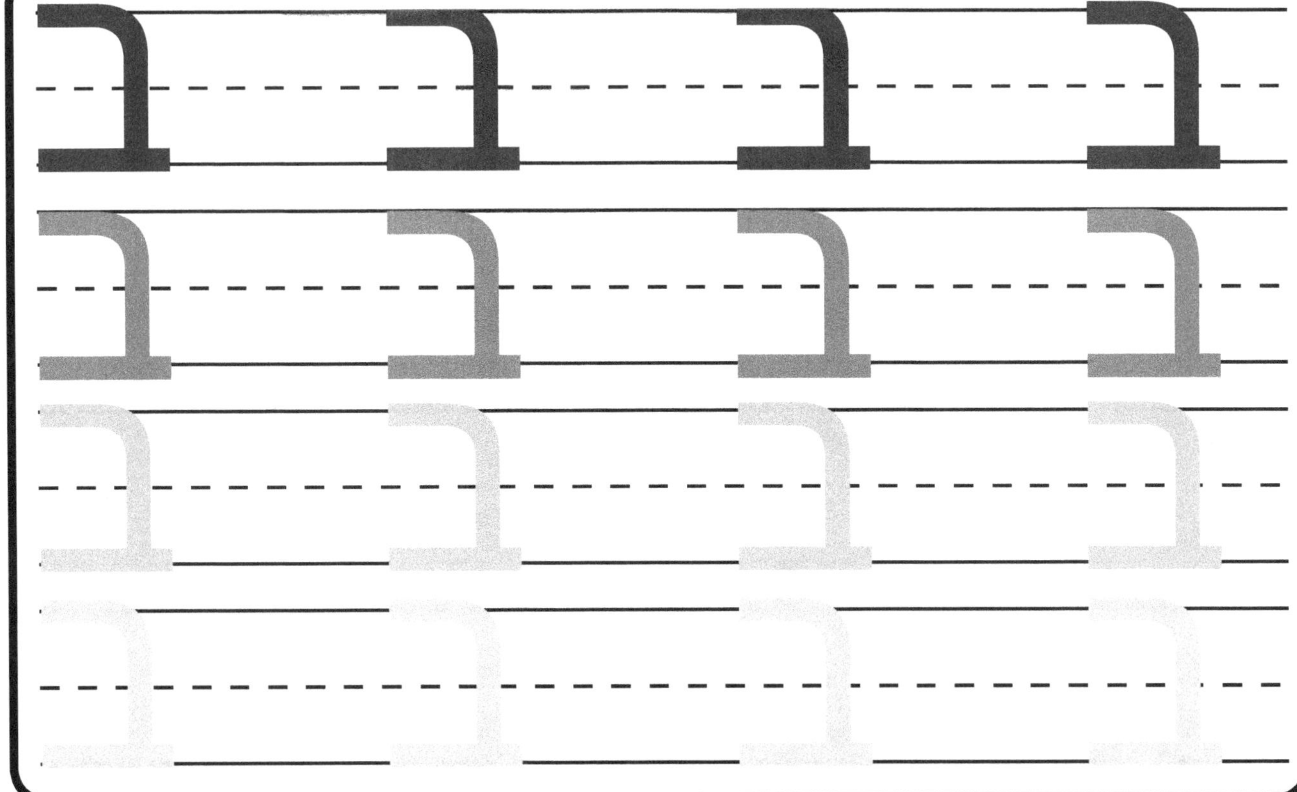

GIMMEL

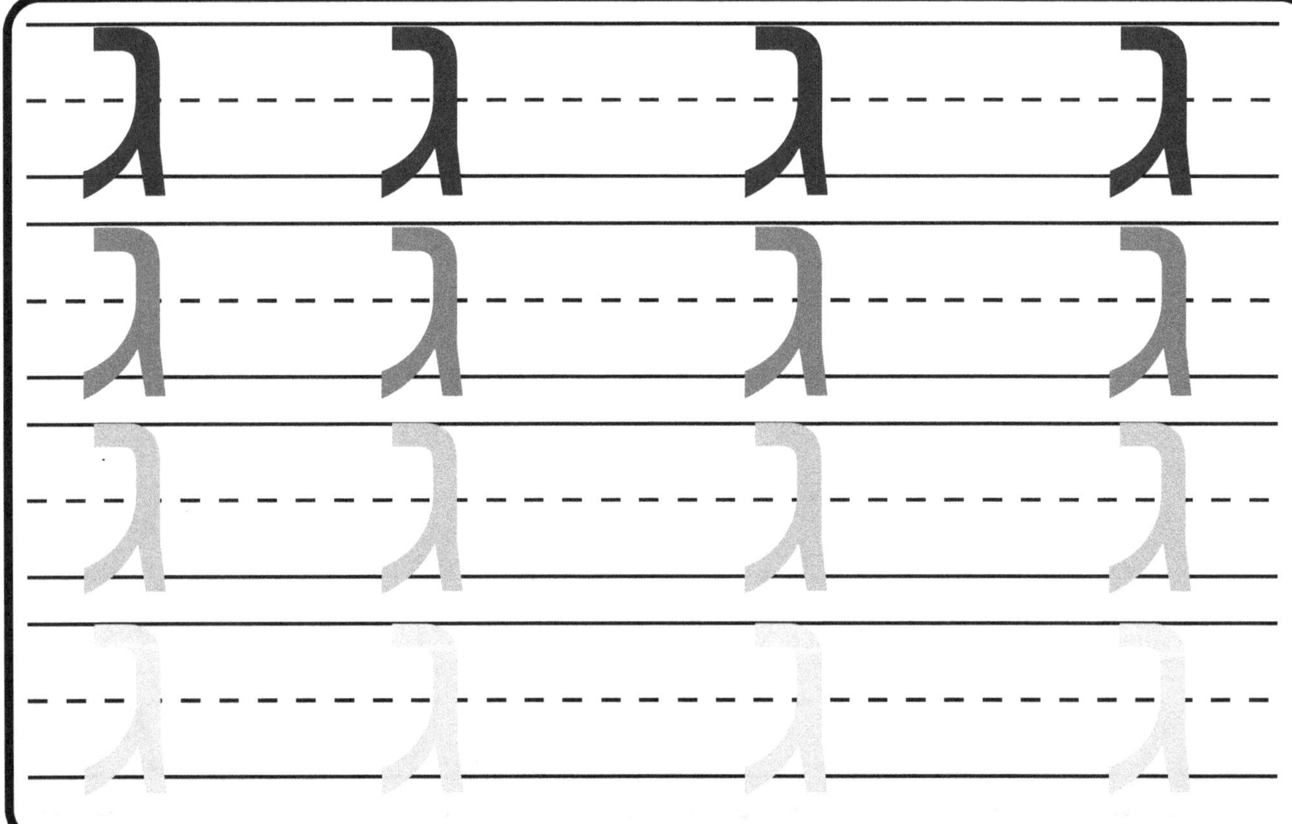

DALED

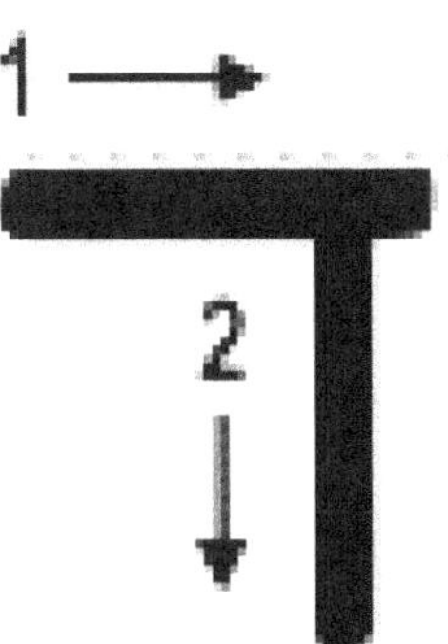

HAY

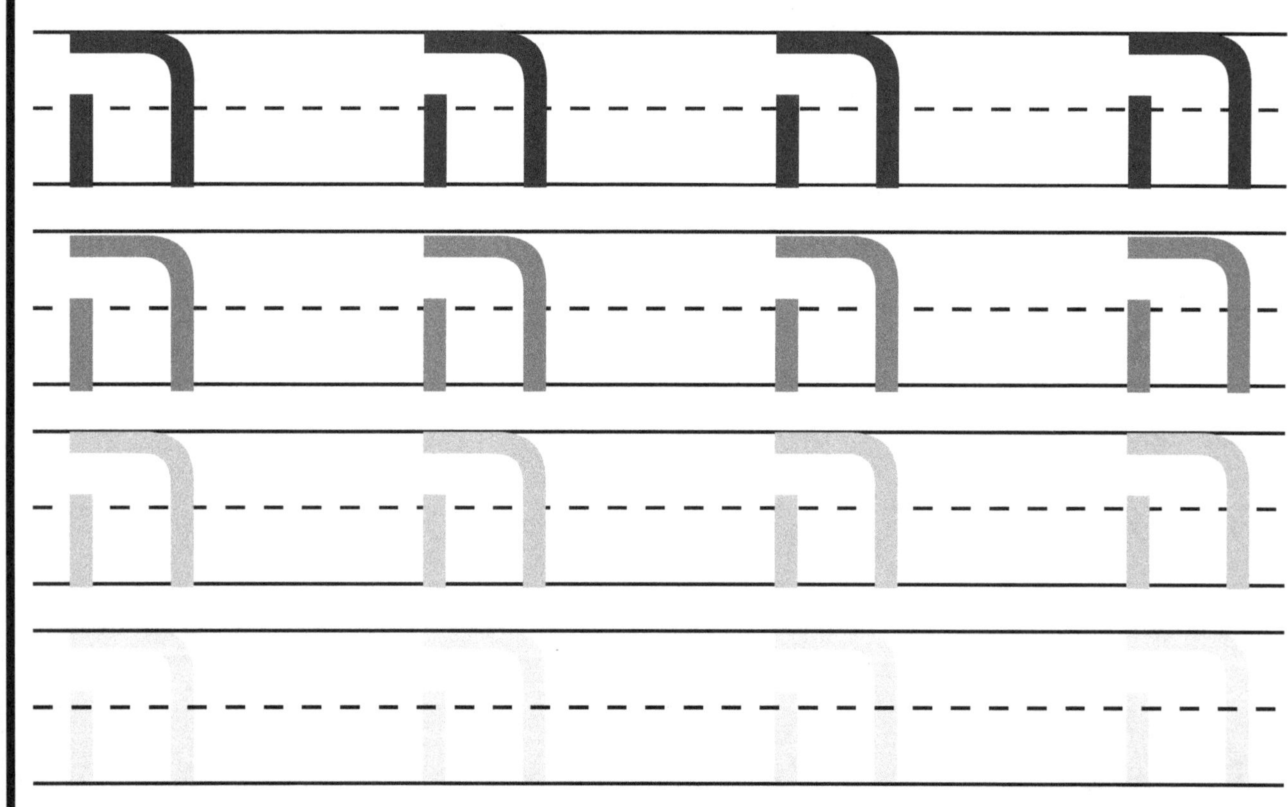

VAV

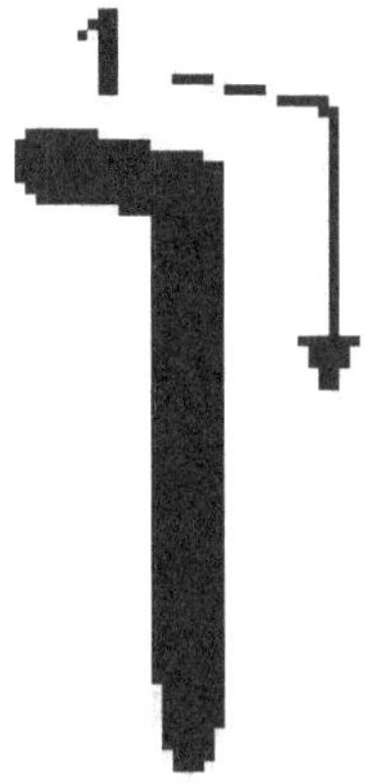

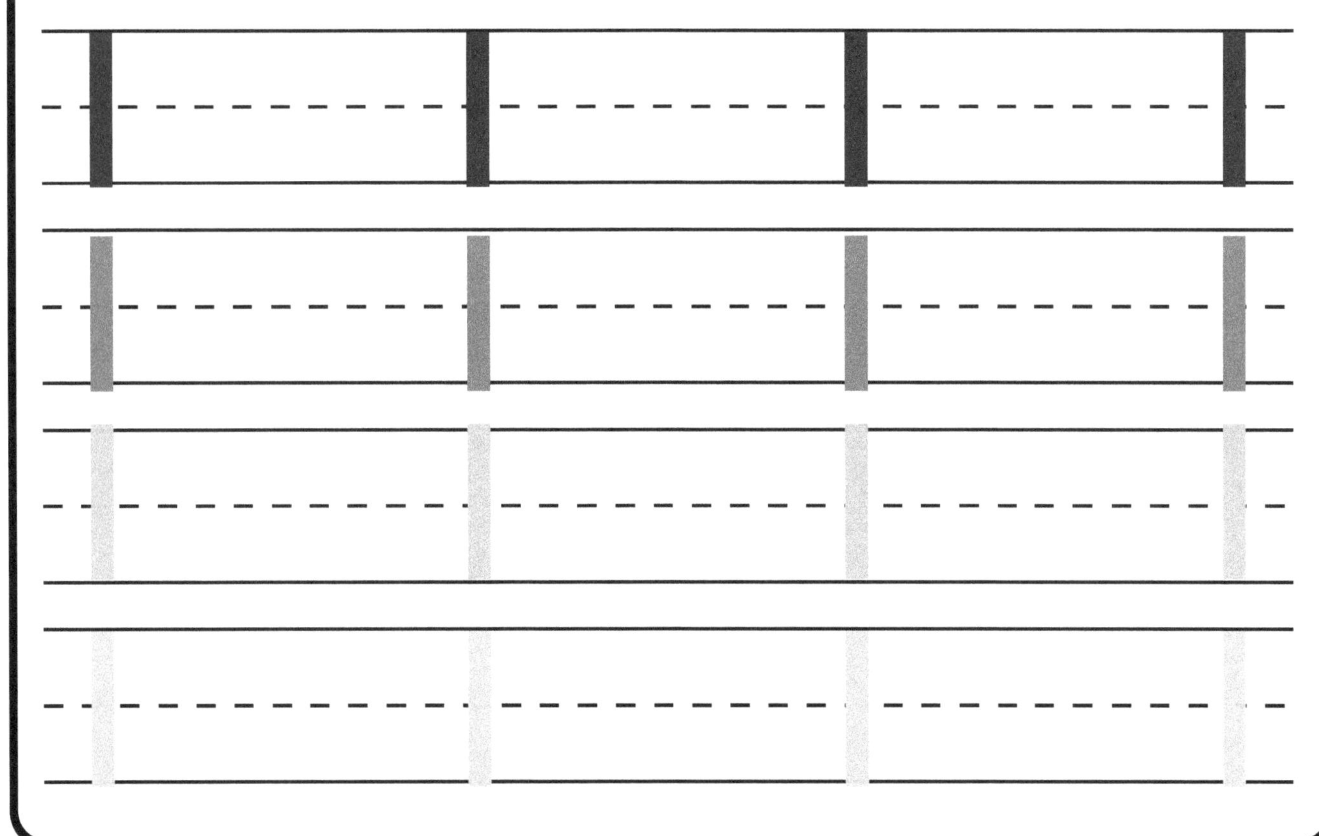

ZAYIN

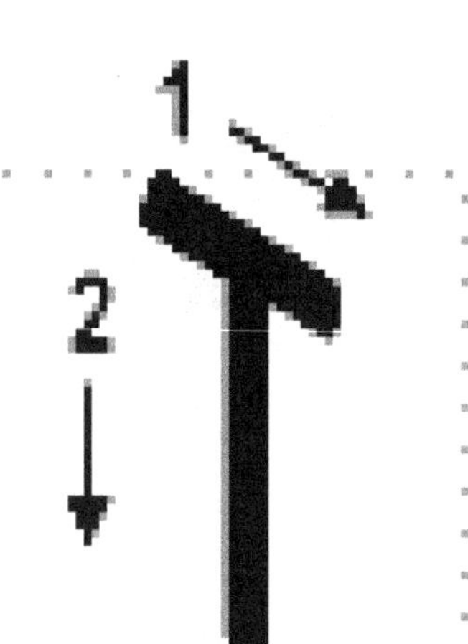

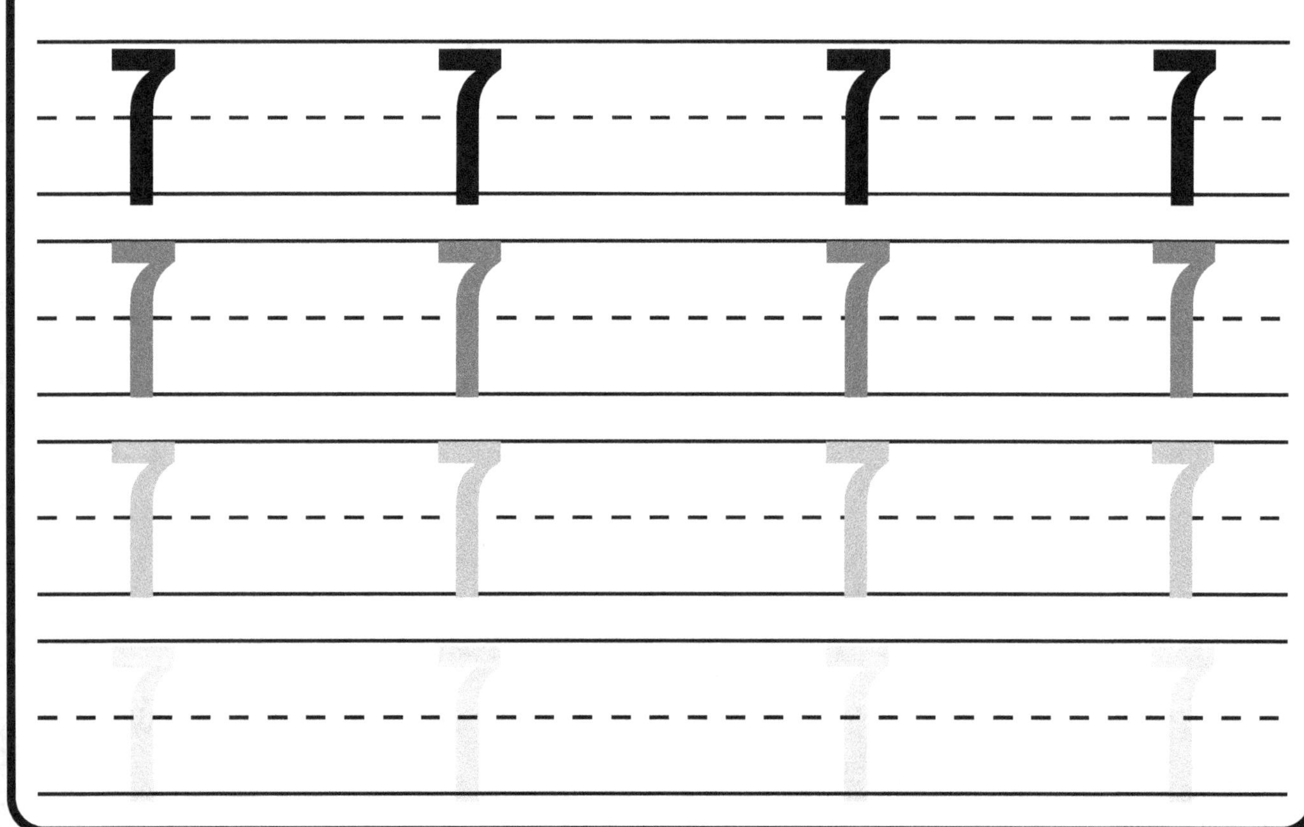

CHET

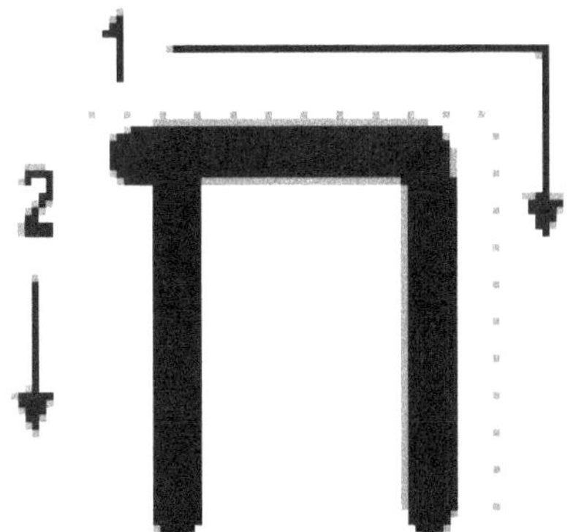

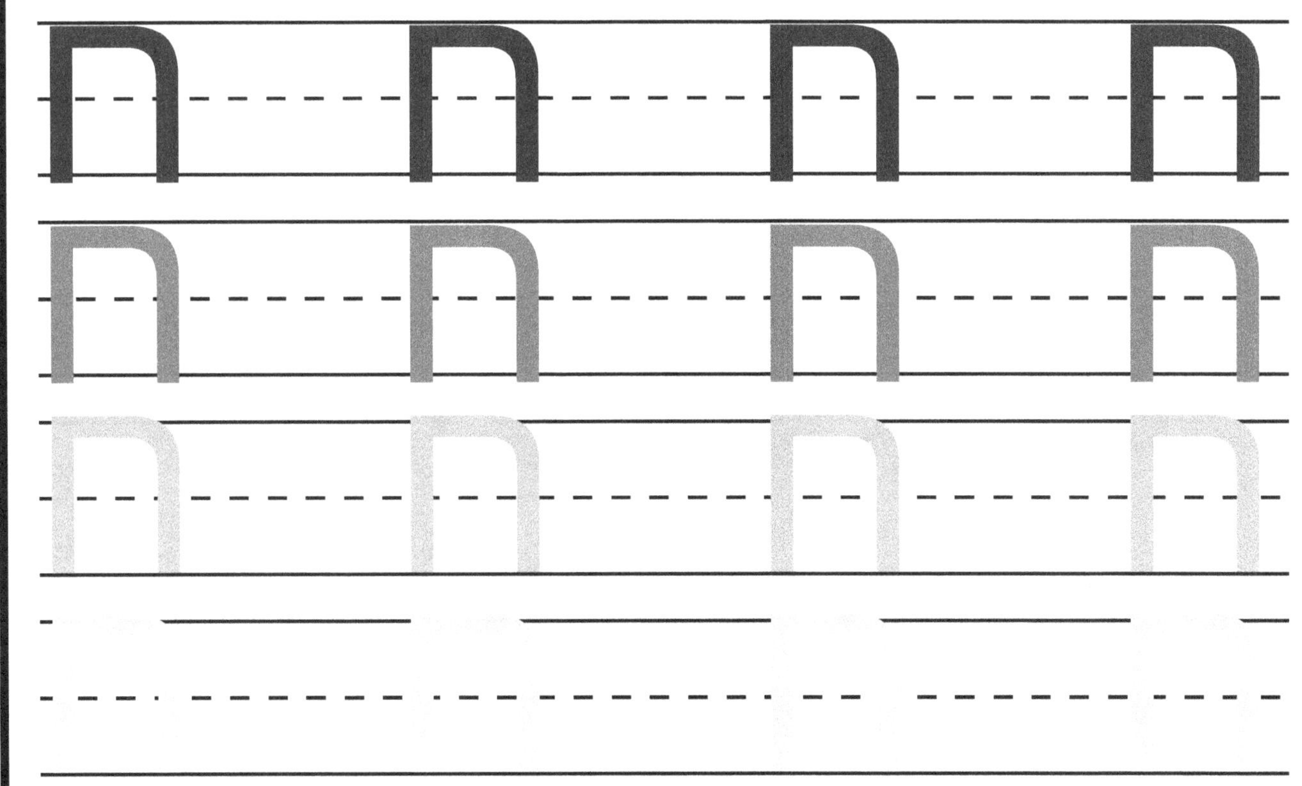

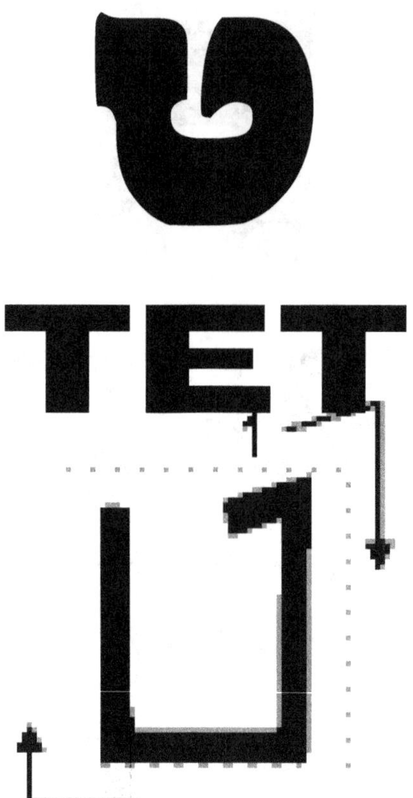

TET

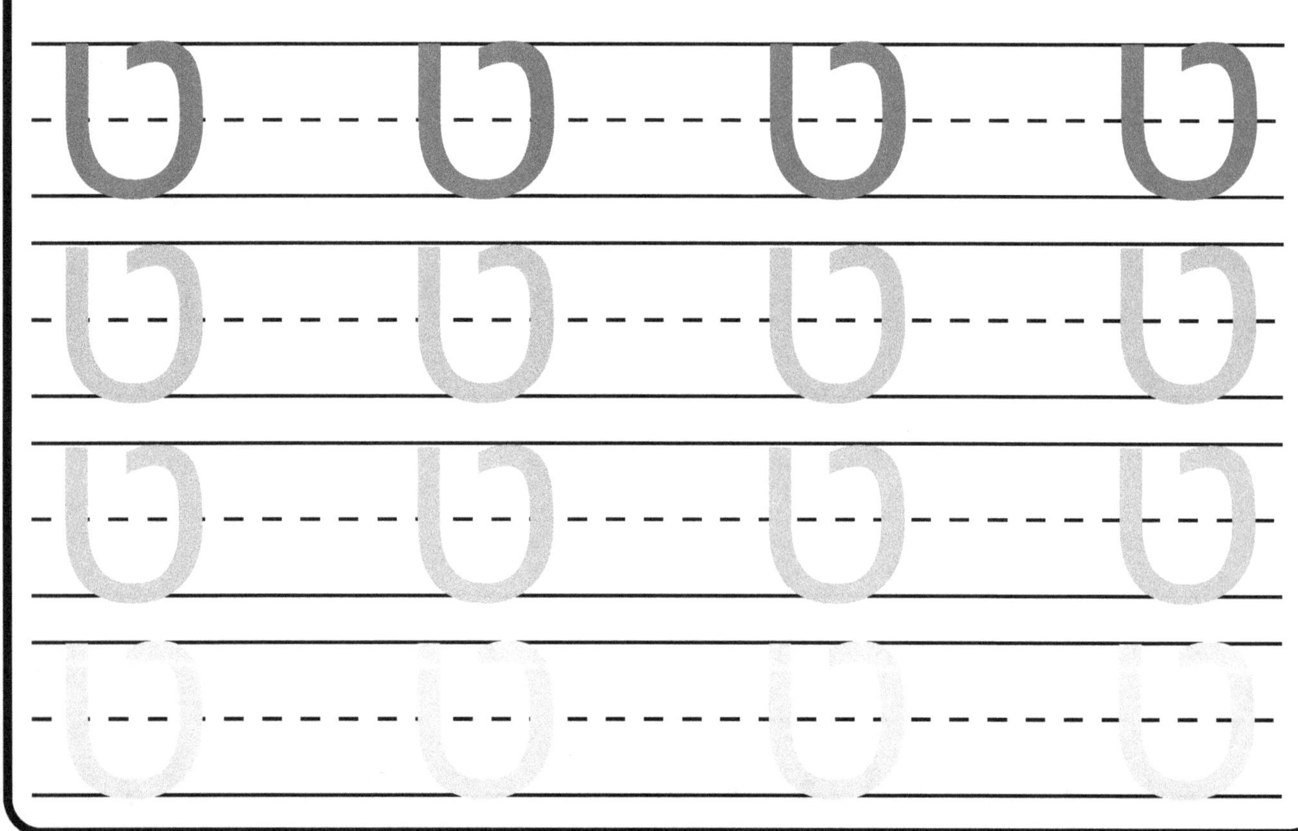

YUD

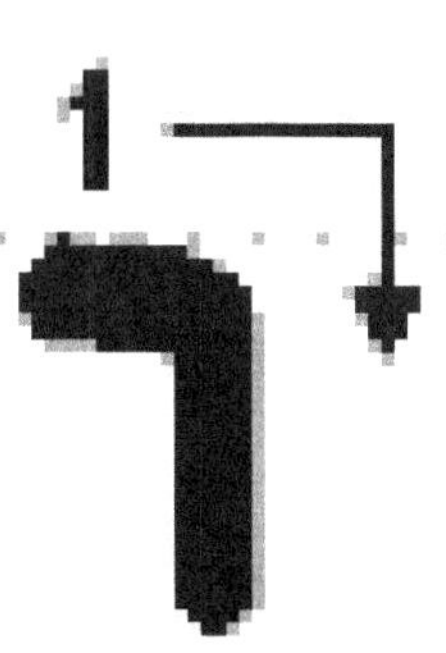

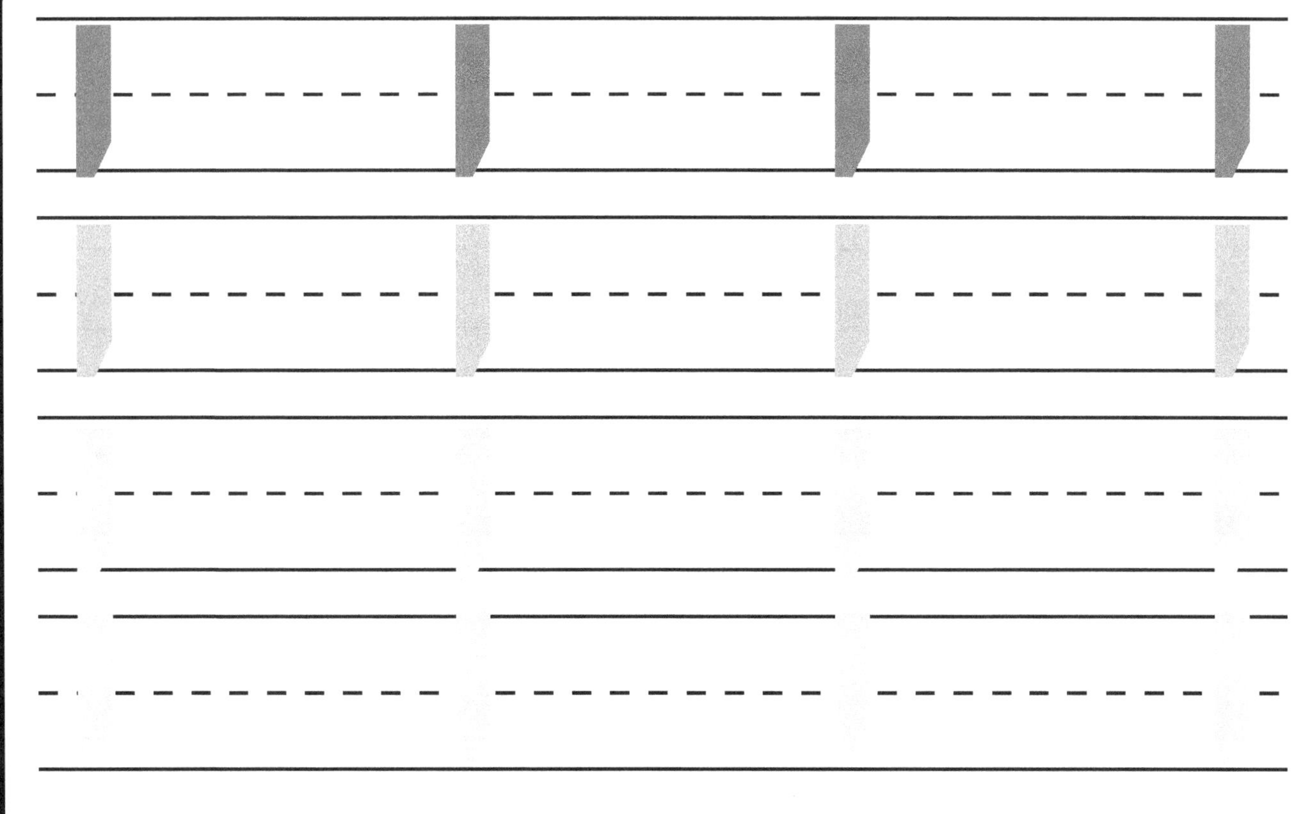

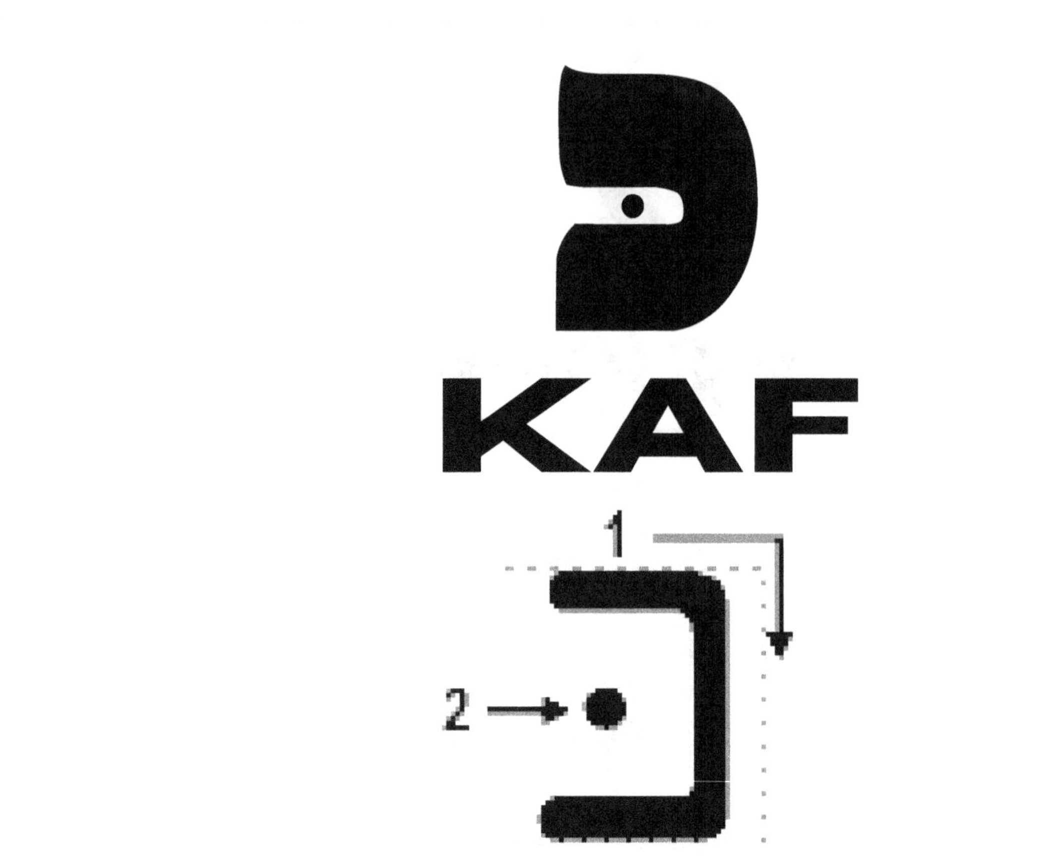
KAF
1
2

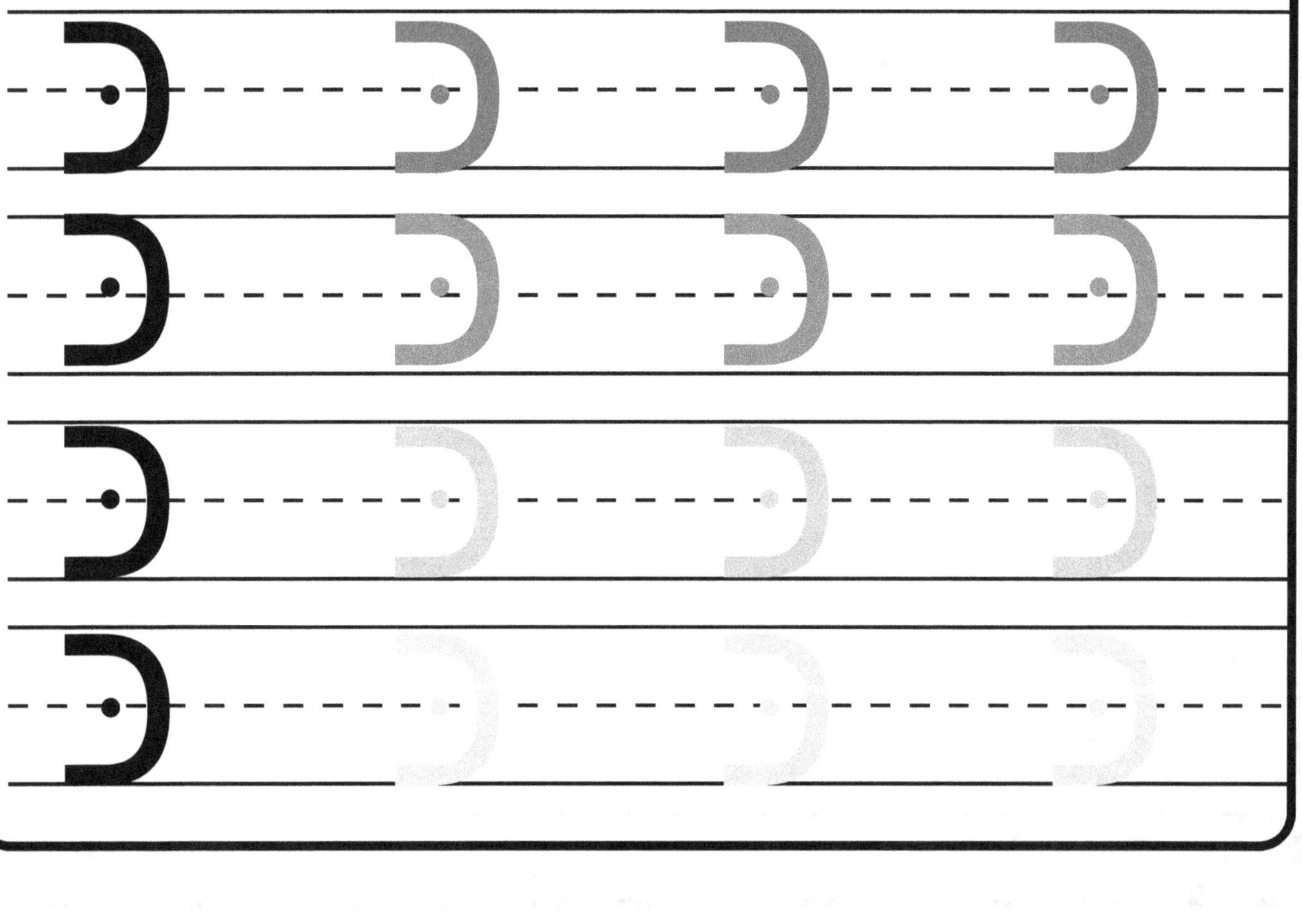

KHAF

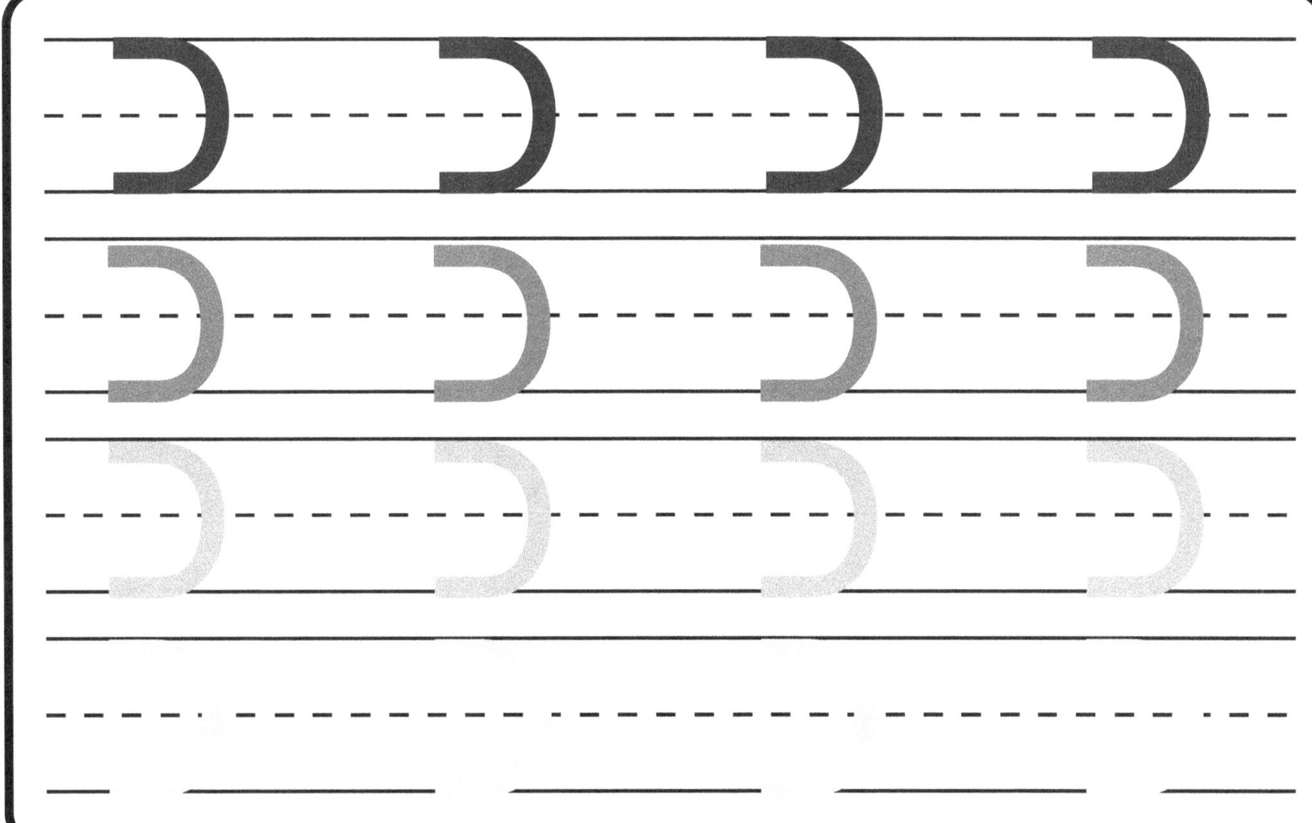

FINAL CHAF

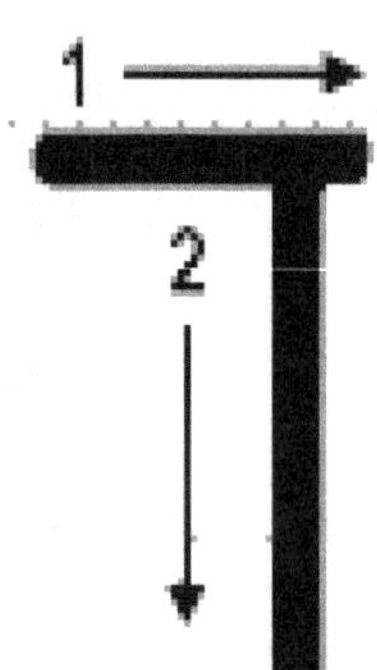

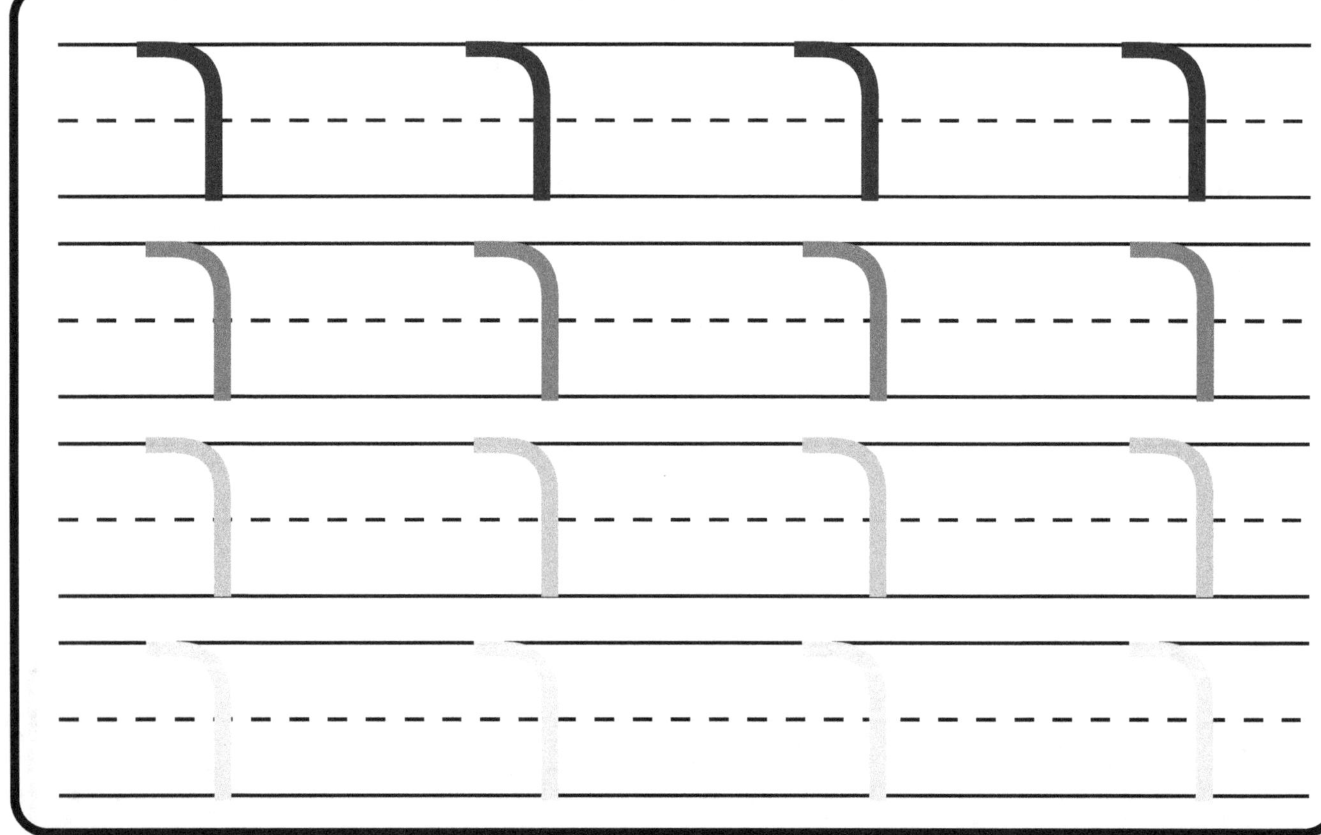

LAMED

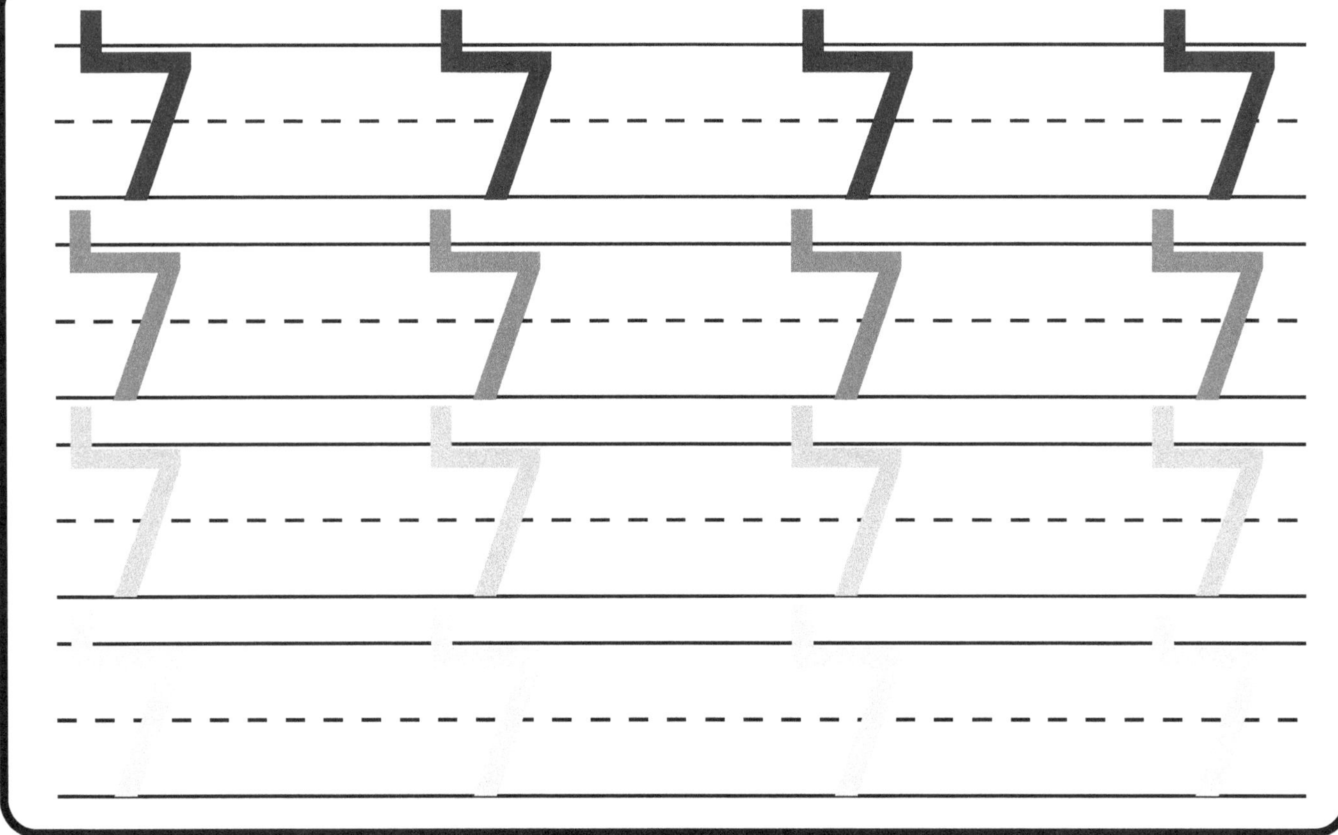

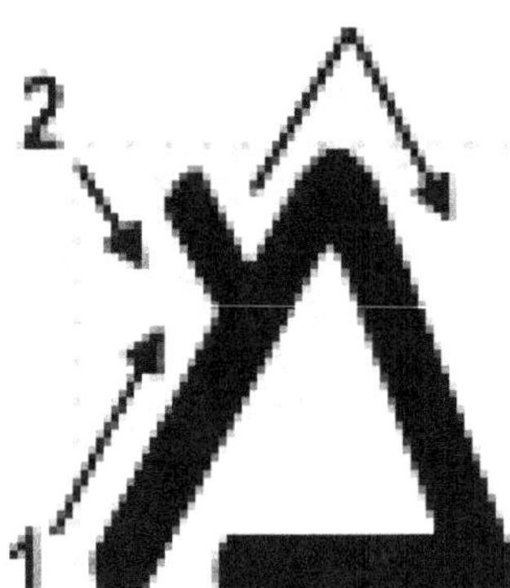

MEM

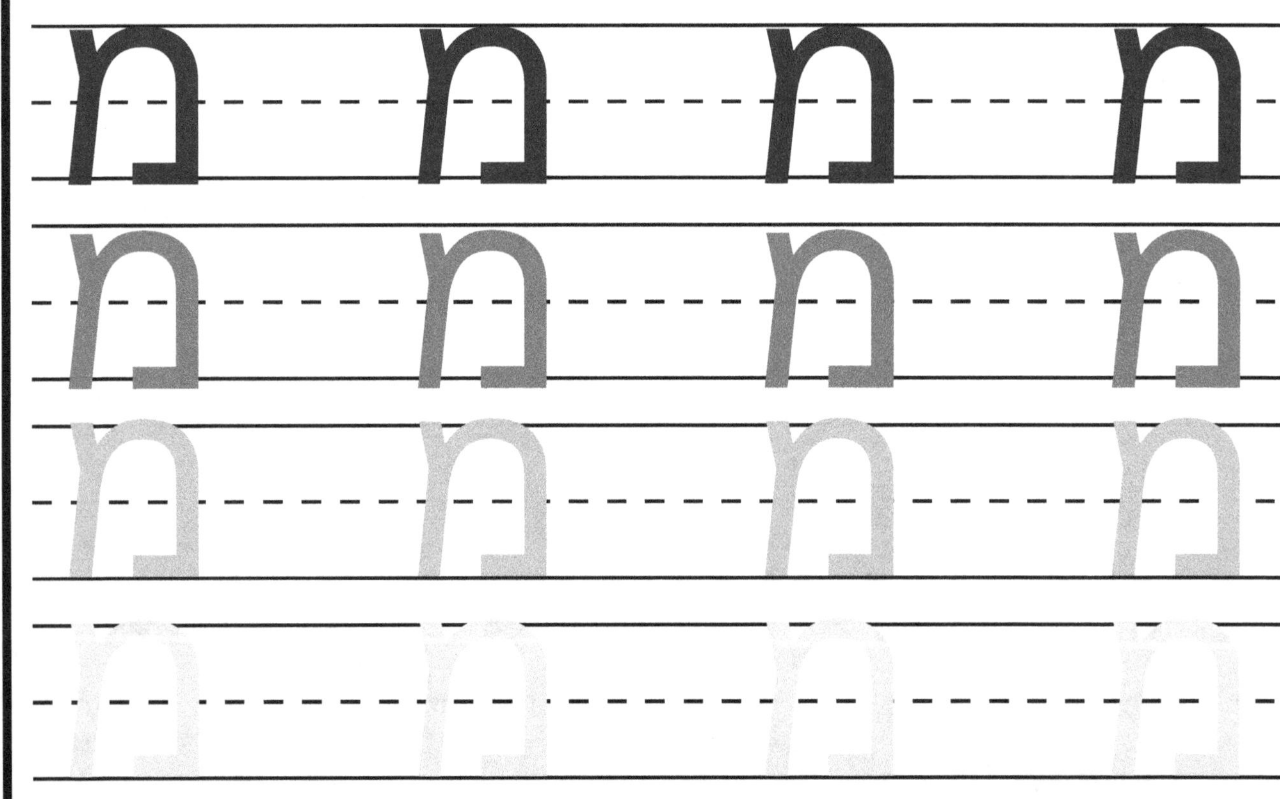

FINAL MEM

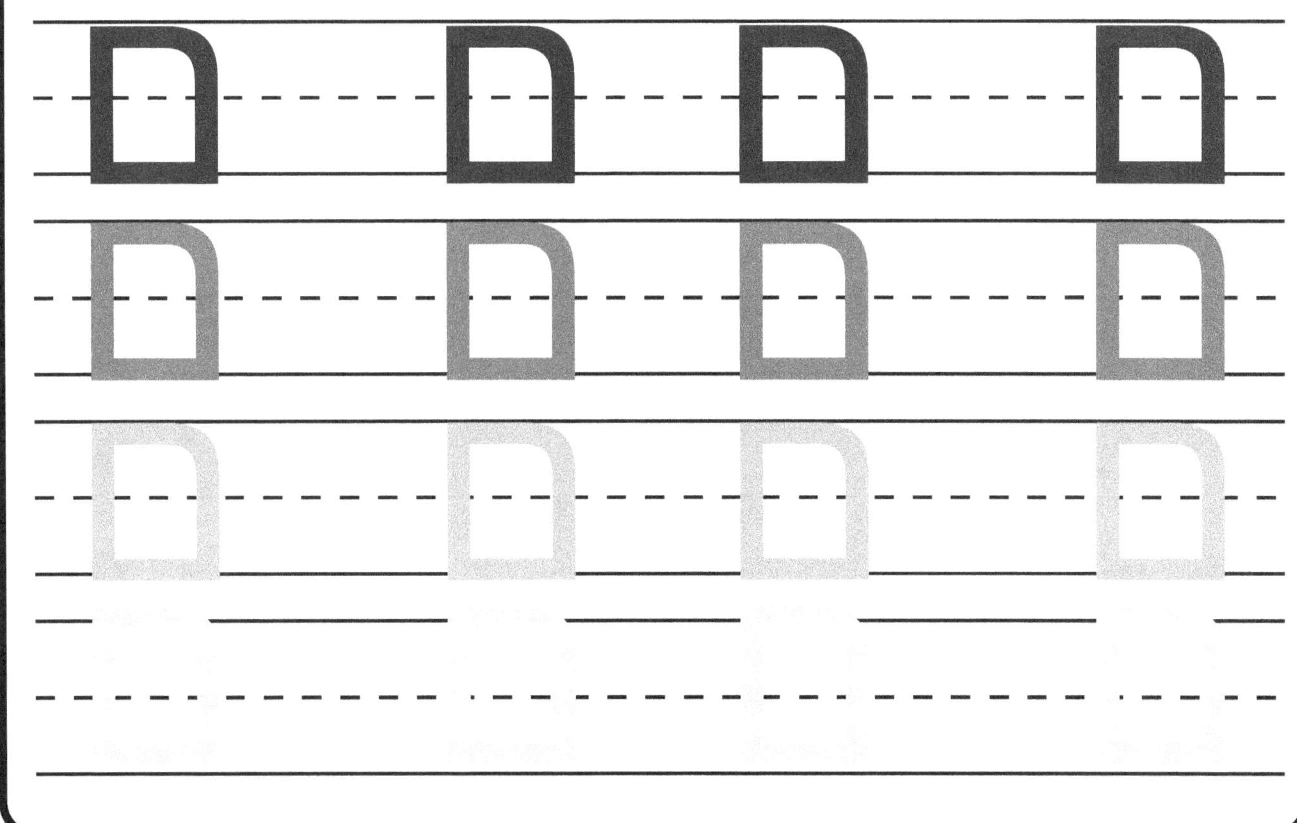

נ

NUN

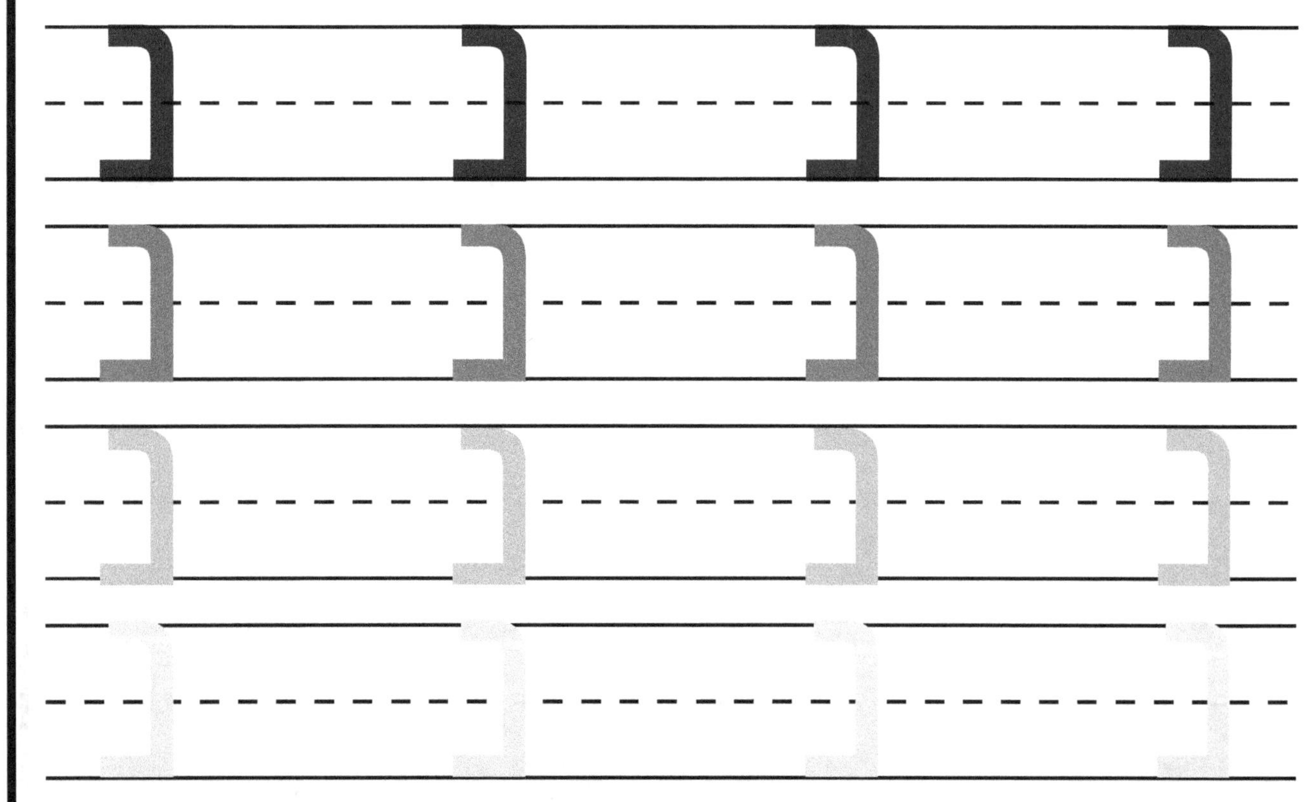

FINAL
NUN

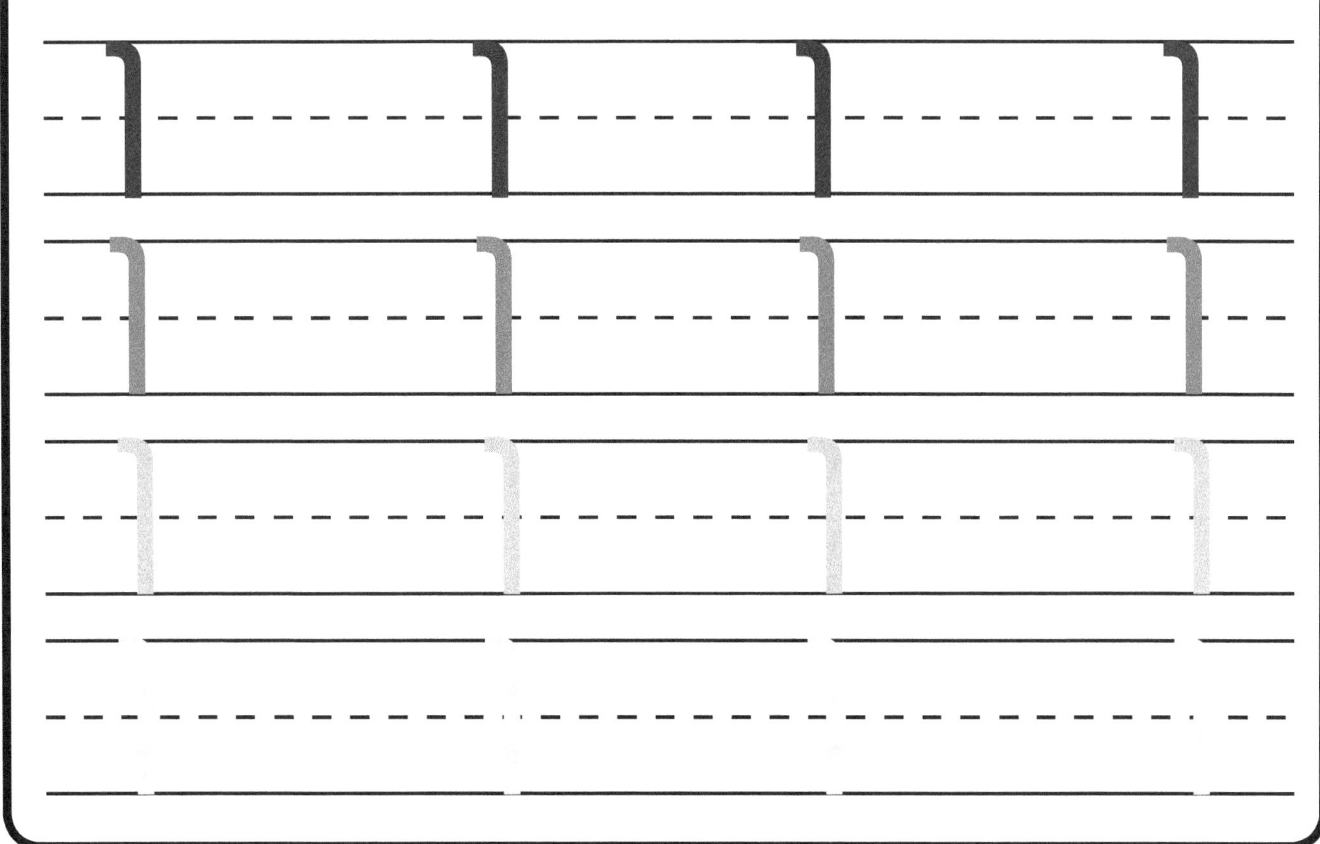

SAMECH

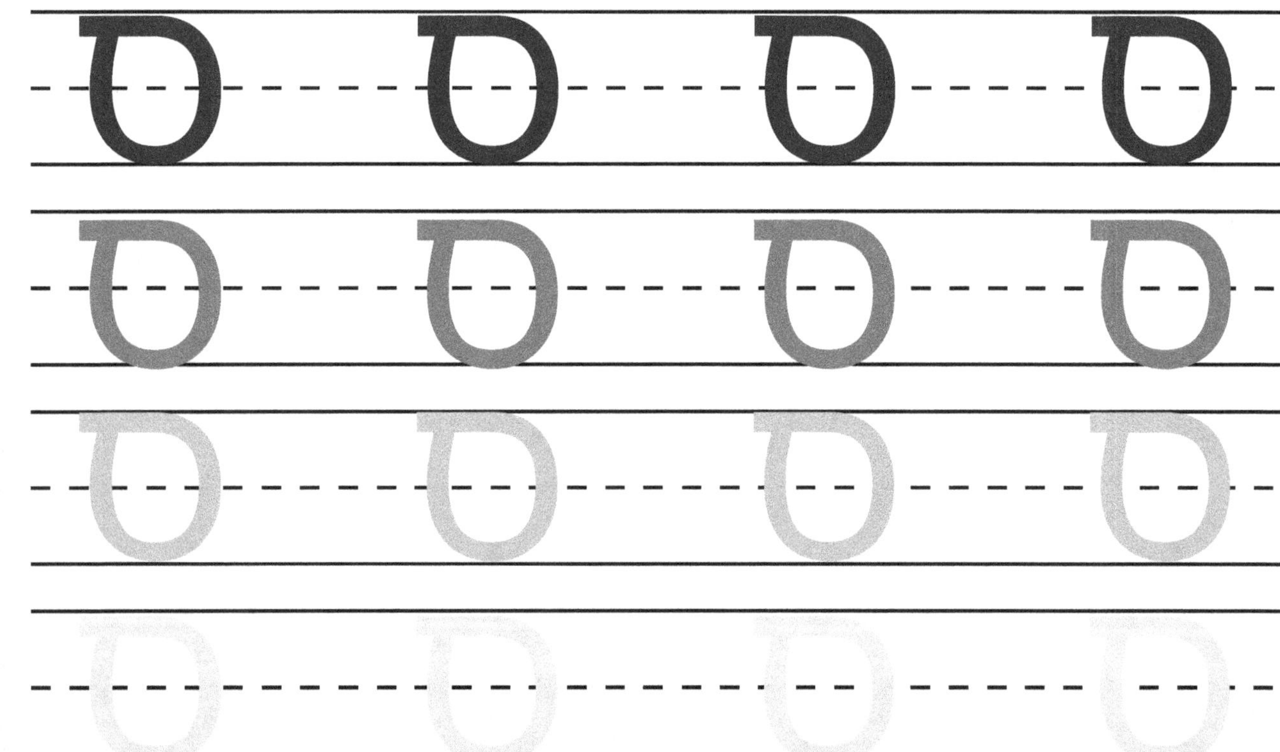

AYIN

ע

PAY

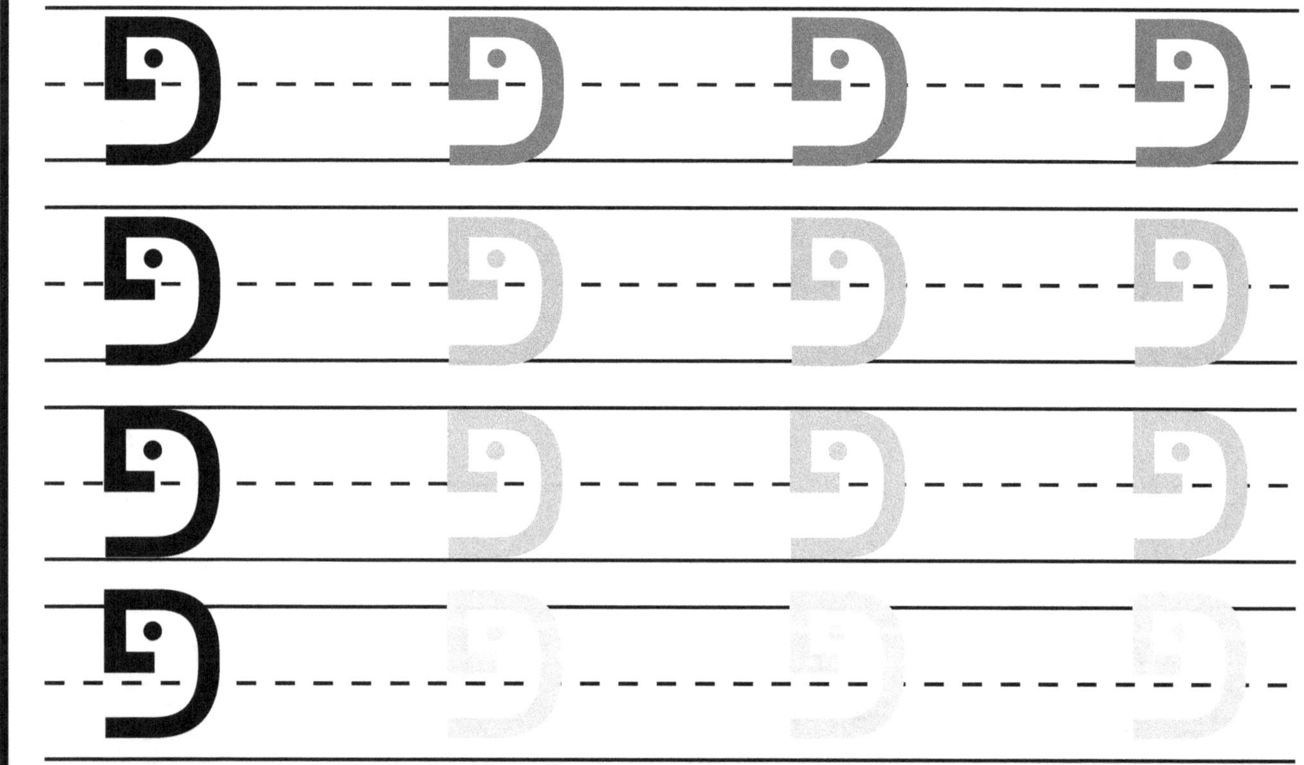

FAY

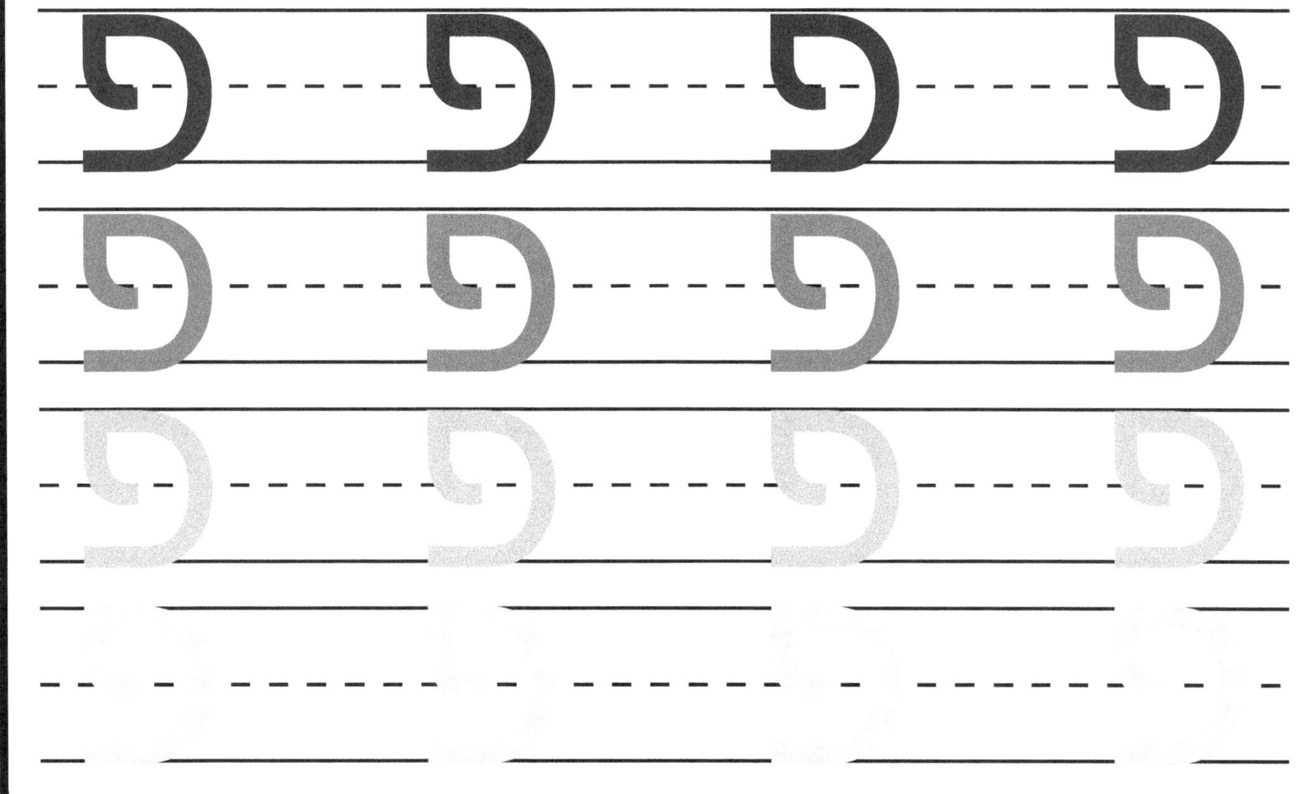

FINAL FAY

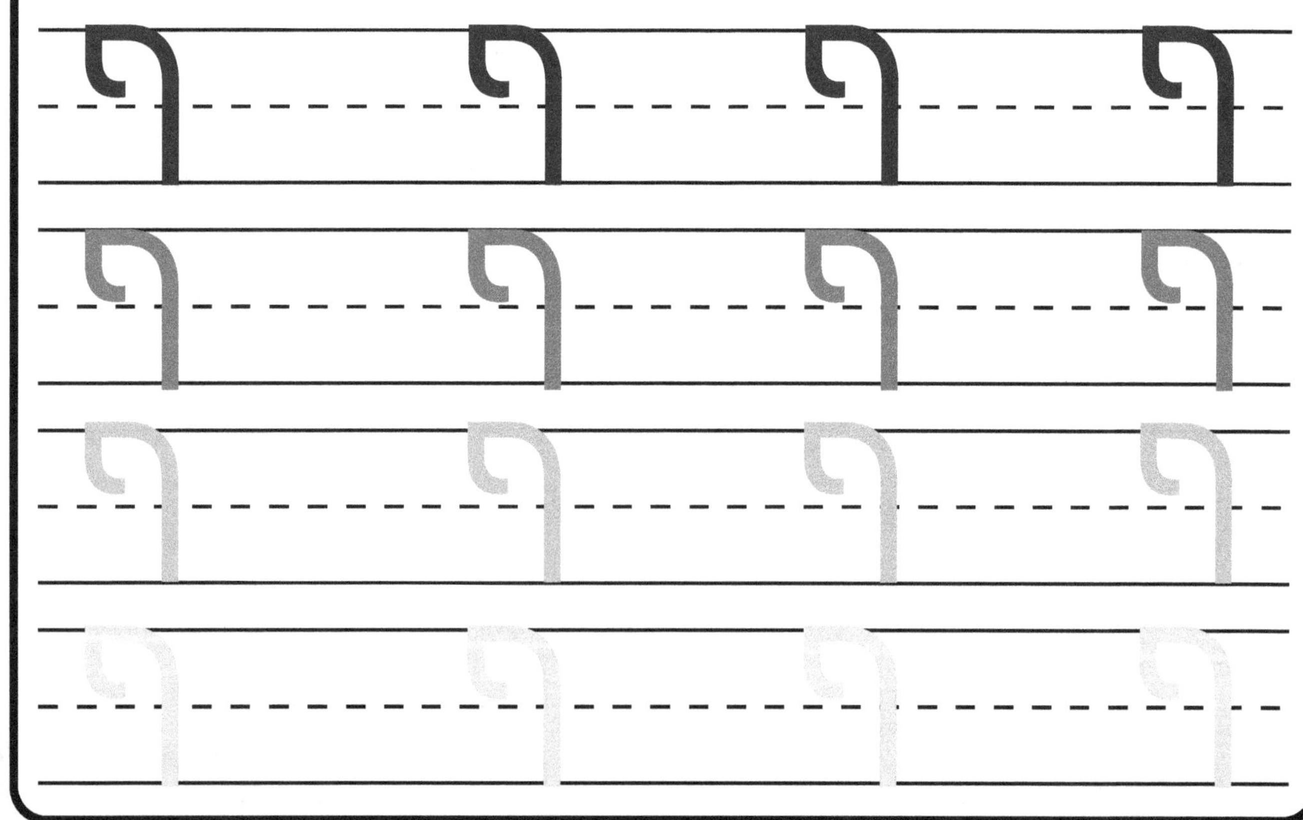

TZADI

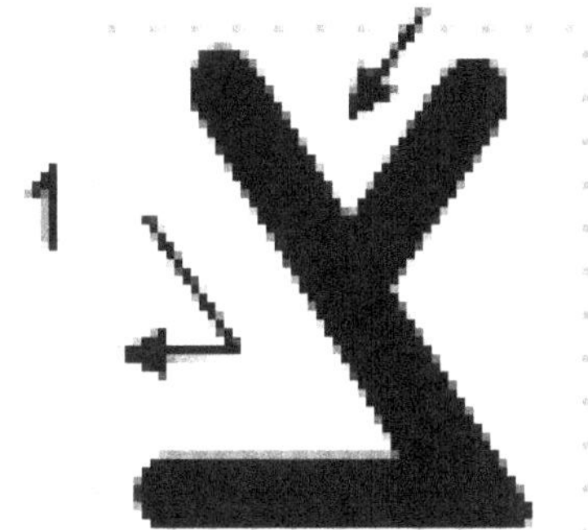

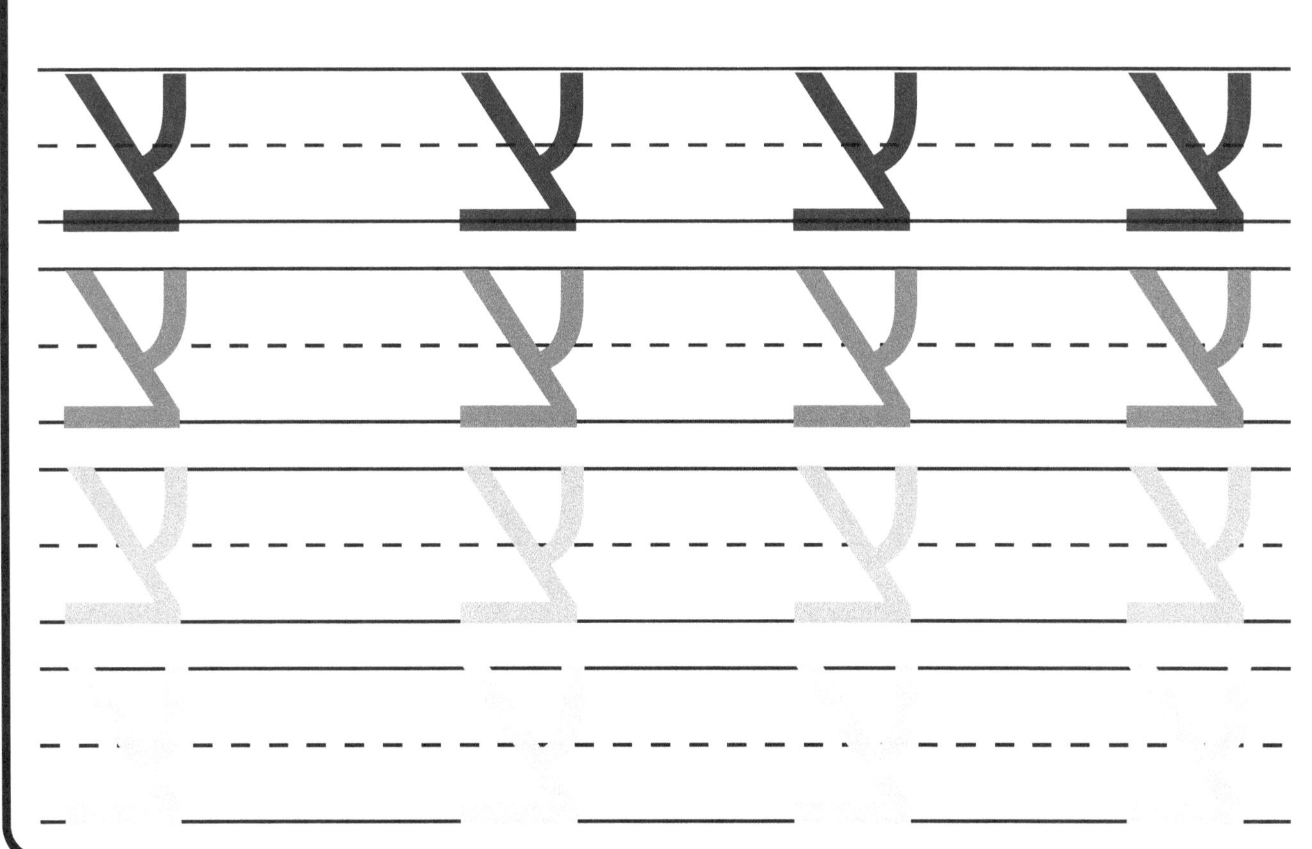

FINAL TZADI

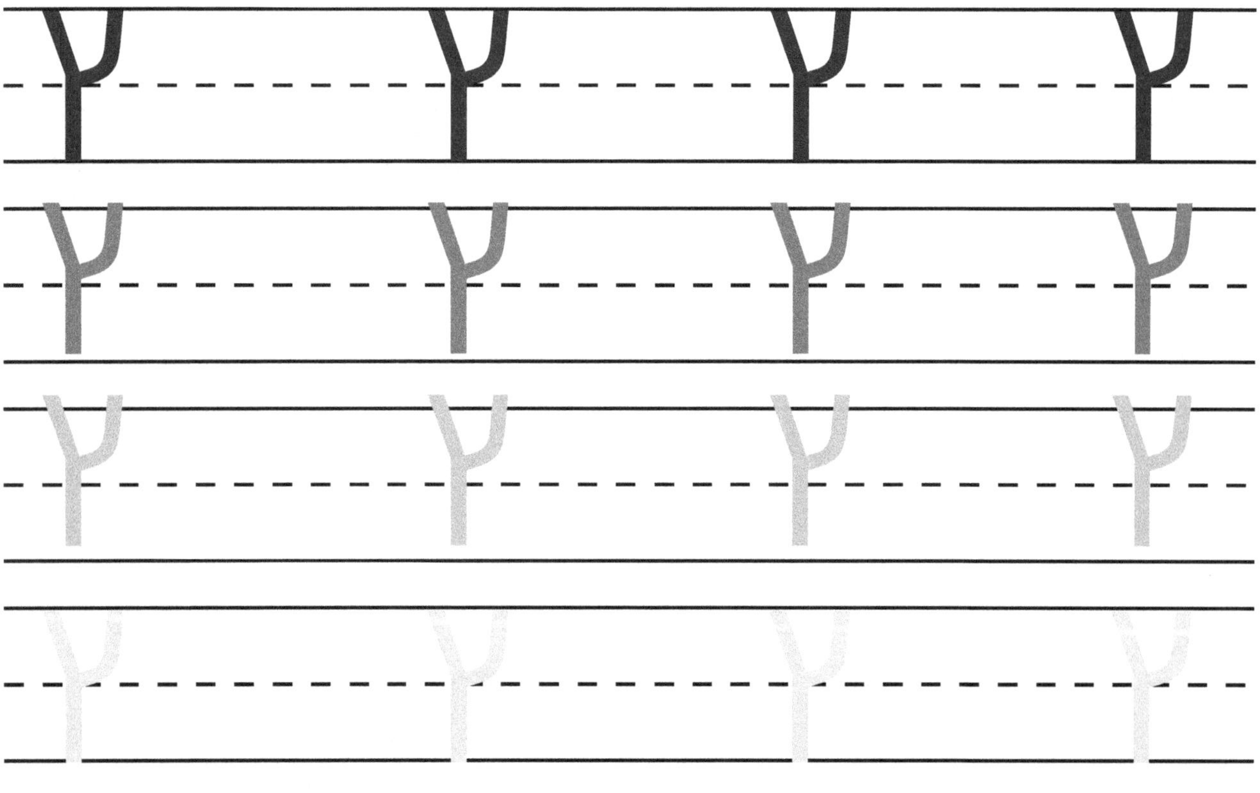

KOOF

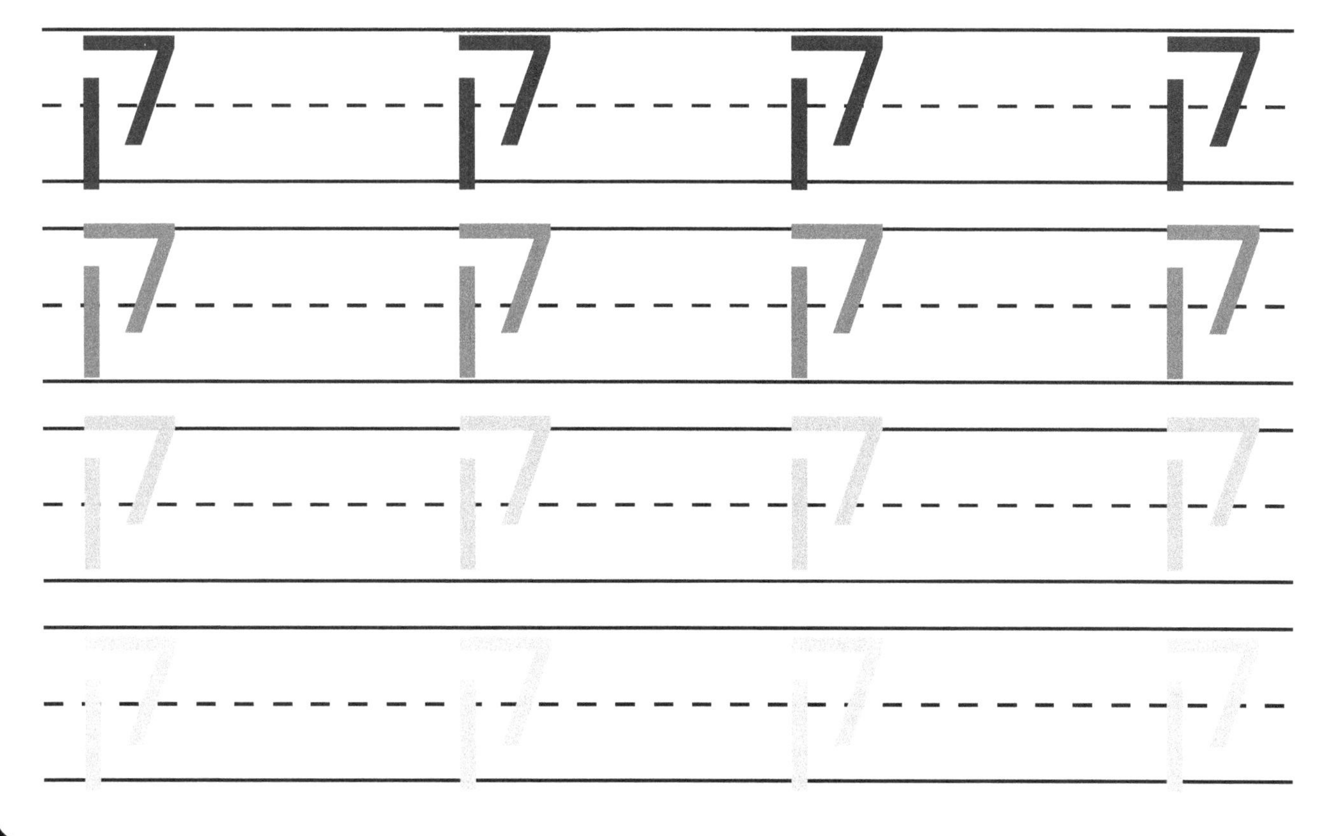

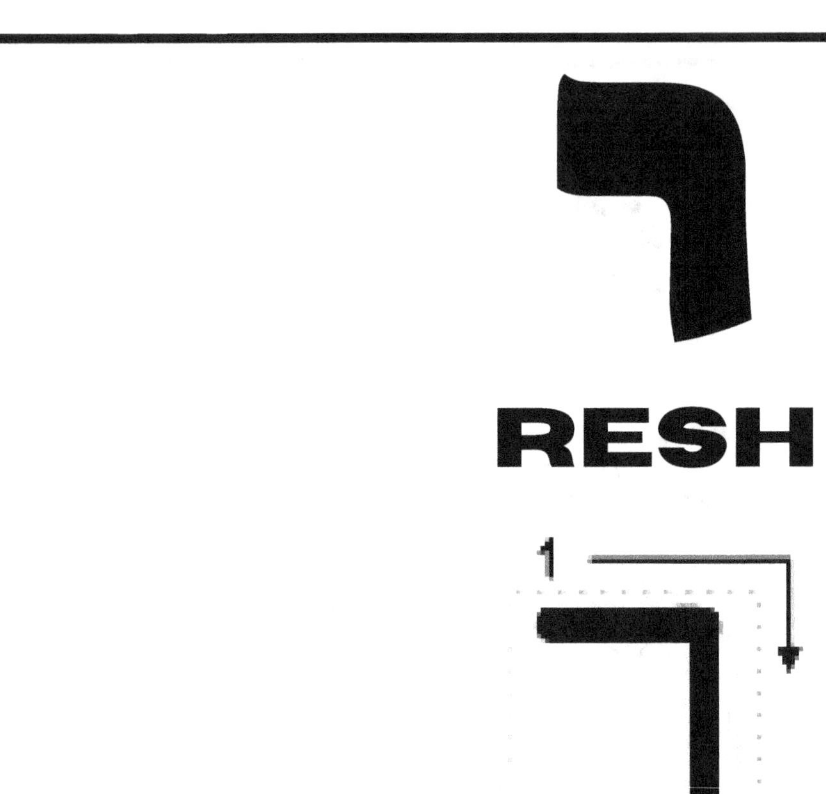

RESH

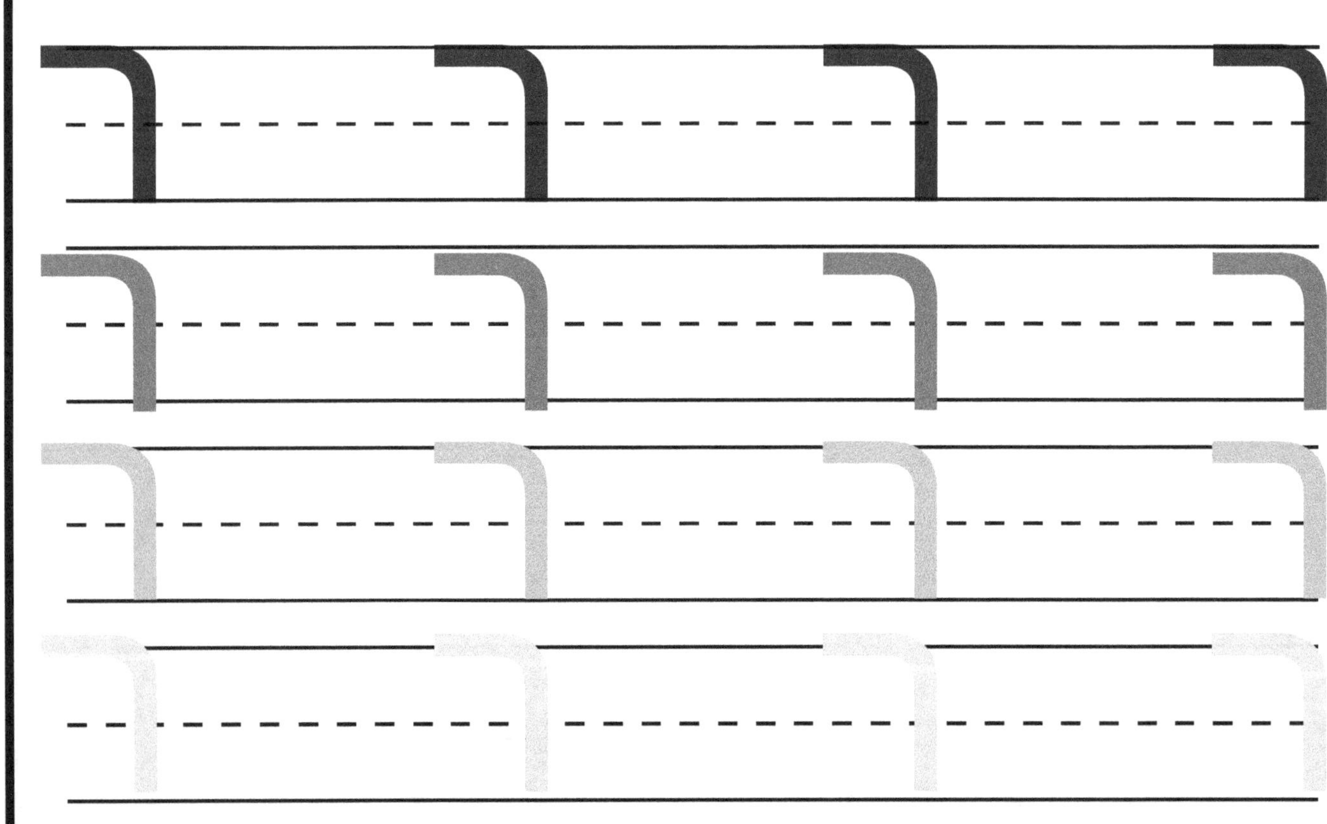

SHIN

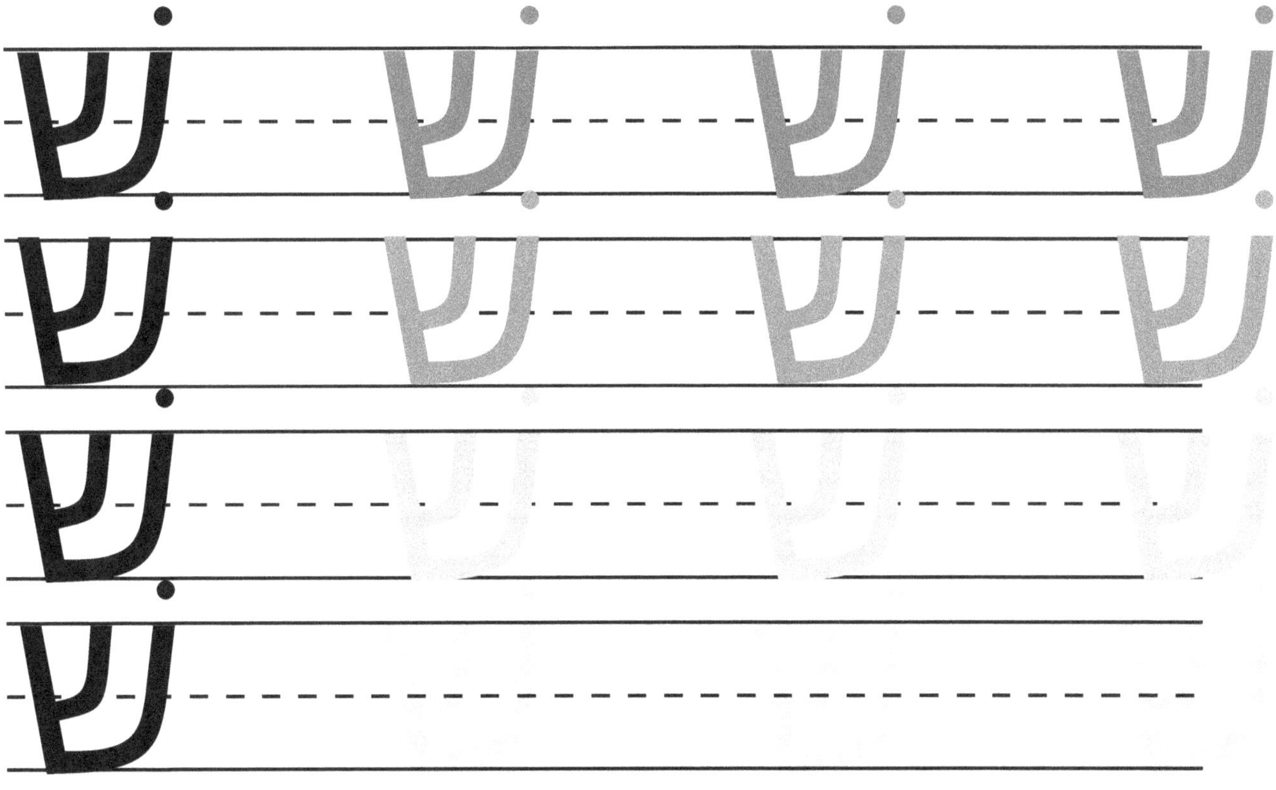

שׂ
SIN

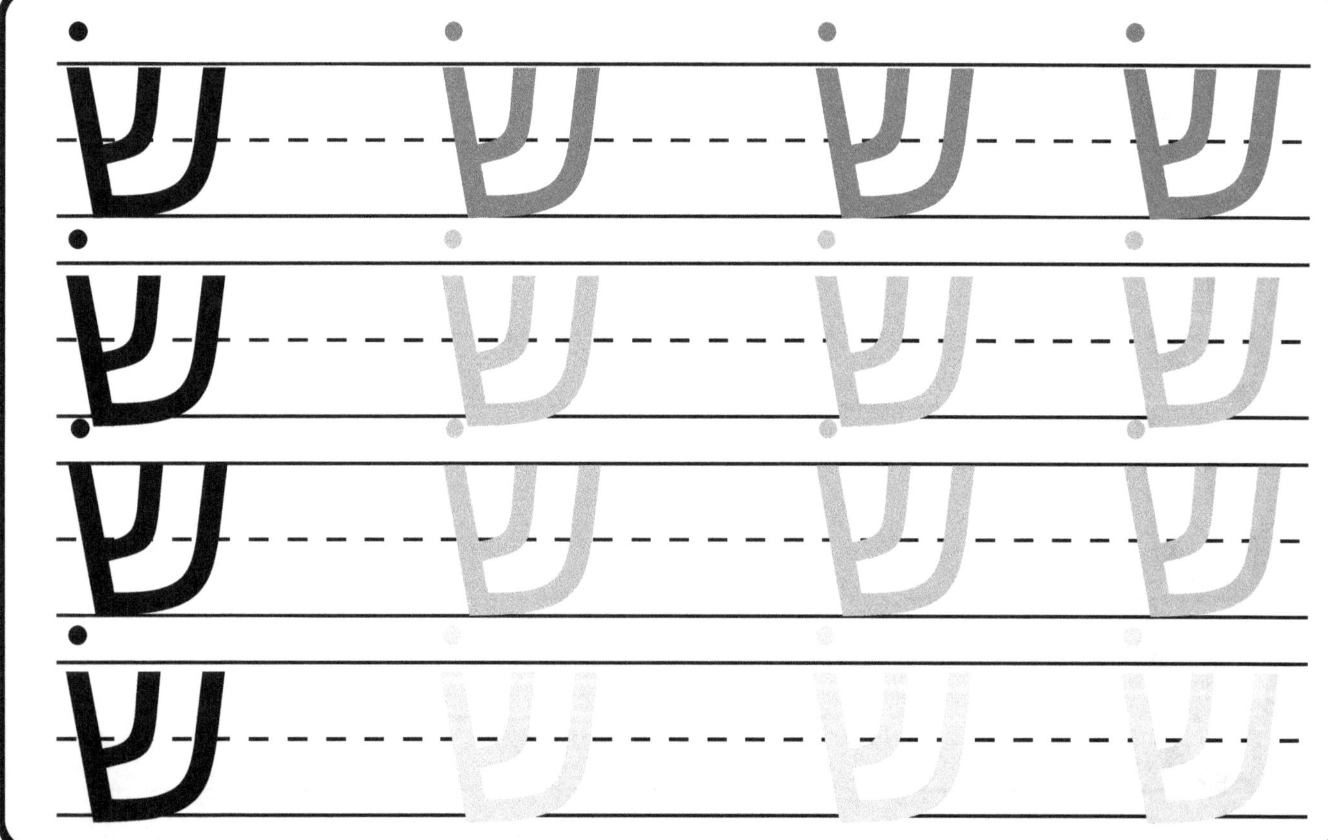

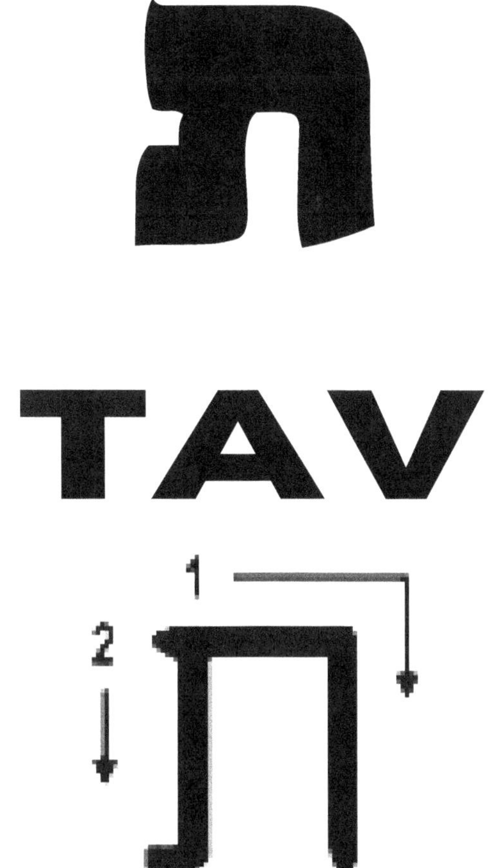

TAV

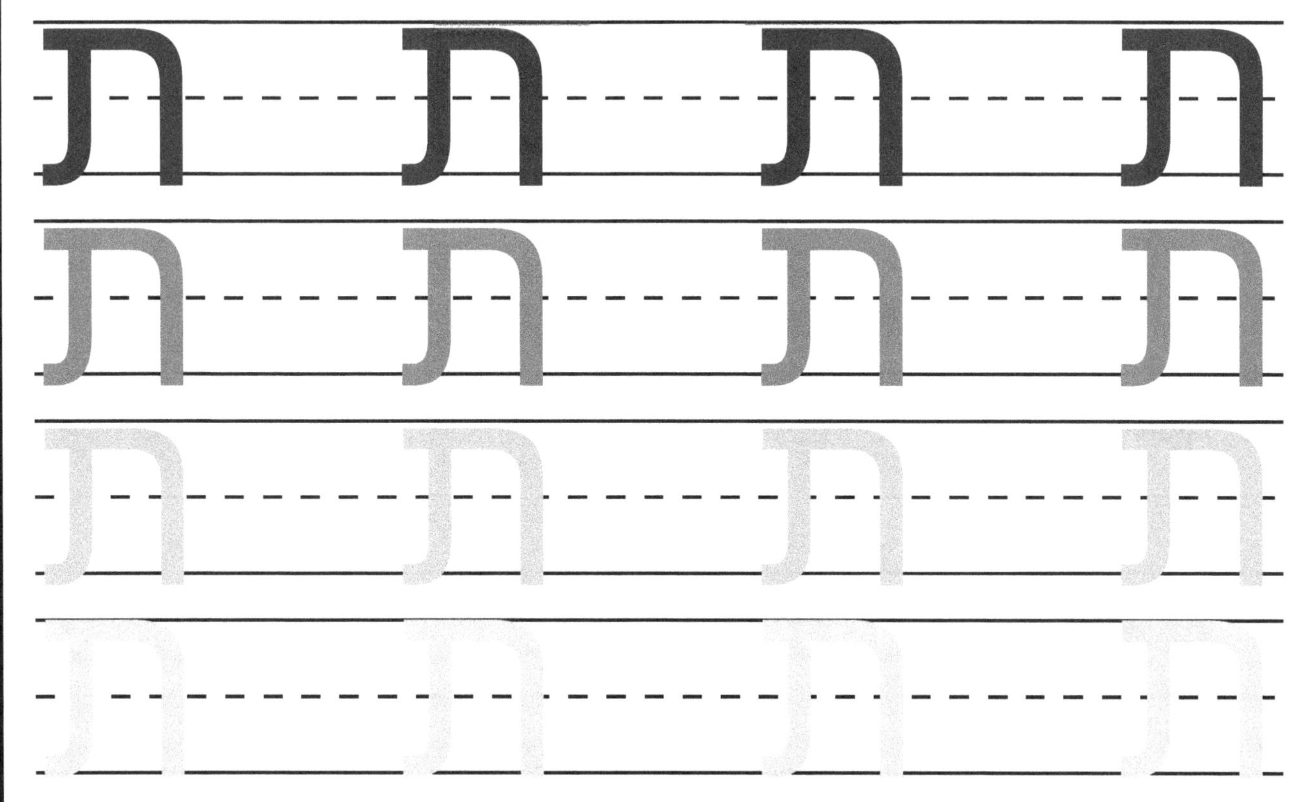

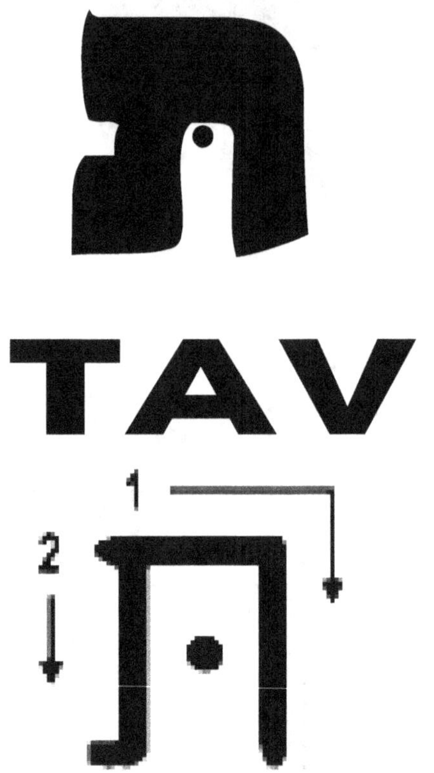

TAV

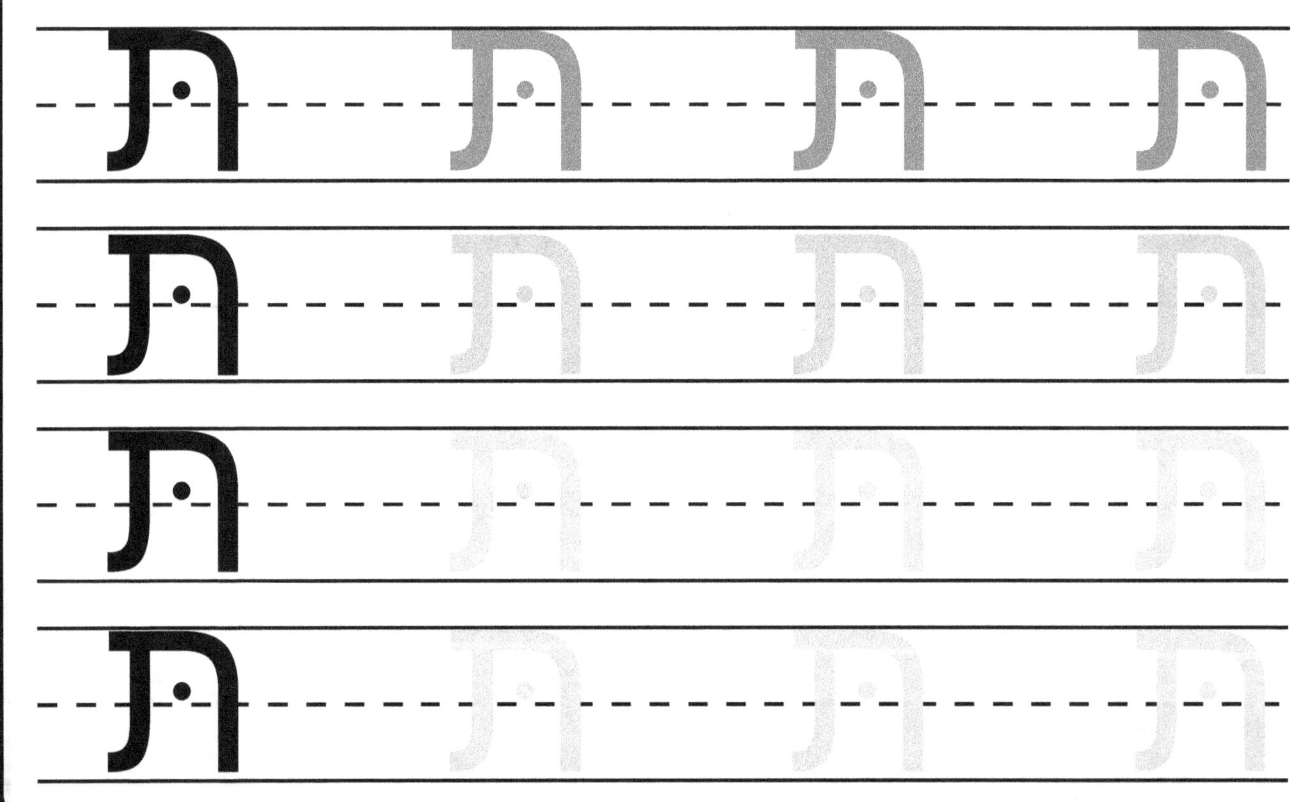

ALEF

אריה

בּ

BET

ברווז

בּ

VET

בַּיִת

GIMMEL

ג'ירפה

DALED

דינוזאור

HAY

היפופוטם

ו

VAV

ורד

ZAYIN

זברה

ח

CHET

חלה

ט

TET

טלה

׳

YUD

ילדים

כ

KAF

כדורגל

כ

KHAF

כסא

FINAL
CHAF

ל

LAMED

ליצן

מ

MEM

מספריים

n n n n n

FINAL
MEM

סוס

D

נ

NUN

נעליים

FINAL
NUN

SAMECH

ע

AYIN

עוגה

פינגווין

פ

FAY

פרח

FINAL
FAY

צ

TZADI

צפרדע

FINAL TZADI

ק

KOOF

קוביות

17

RESH

SHIN

שעון

שׂ

SIN

שועל

ת

TAV

תפוח

TAV

תוכי

keep our language

LIFE FOR EVER

by wolfeyesqueen